DEVOTIONS®

December

❧ Looking forward to the city with foundations, whose architect and builder is God.

—*Hebrews 11:10*

Gary Allen, Editor   **Margaret Williams,** Project Editor   Photo © Liquid Library

DEVOTIONS® is published quarterly by Standard Publishing, Cincinnati, Ohio, www.standardpub.com. © 2010 by Standard Publishing. All rights reserved. Topics based on the Home Daily Bible Readings, International Sunday School Lessons. © 2008 by the Committee on the Uniform Series. Printed in the U.S.A. All Scripture quotations, unless otherwise indicated, are taken from the HOLY BIBLE, *NEW INTERNATIONAL VERSION*®. *NIV*®. Copyright © 1973, 1978, 1984 by Biblica, Inc.™. Used by permission of Zondervan. All rights reserved. *King James Version* (KJV), public domain.

Shine the Light

Listen to me, my people; hear me, my nation: The law will go out from me; my justice will become a light to the nations (Isaiah 51:4).

Scripture: Isaiah 51:1-6
Song: "Let the Light Stream In"

As I enjoyed a watercolor painting, I marveled at how narrow lines of white space defined people and objects. I've dabbled in watercolor, so I know how hard it is to leave such margins. The paint may run. And then the painting may look amateurish if the white spaces aren't properly blended into the whole. Yet this particular painter used white to make glorious light shine down upon the scene, truly the mark of a talented artist.

Just as the "white" of a painting brings light to a scene, and defines objects, so God's Word brings light to our society in a way that defines morality and justice. Do governments wonder what is right or wrong in a human rights issue? Check God's Word. Do communities wonder what is fair or unfair to residents? Consider God's Word. Do individuals wonder how to treat those with whom they disagree? Consult God's Word.

As I read God's Word each morning, I try to apply His principles to the situations of my life. We need never think any issue is too complicated. God's light shines brightest in the darkest places.

Dear Lord, thank You for revealing Your character to me through Your Word. May those who govern us look to Your wisdom in all things. In Jesus' name, amen.

December 1–4. **Shirley Brosius** lives in Millersburg, Pennsylvania, and is the author of a devotional book. She enjoys reading, walking, and playing games with her five grandchildren.

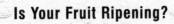

Is Your Fruit Ripening?

Every tree that does not produce good fruit will be cut down and thrown into the fire (Matthew 3:10).

Scripture: Matthew 3:1-10
Song: "I Long to Glorify Thee"

During my college years, I worked on a fruit farm. Each spring we climbed ladders to cull developing peaches, pears, apples, and plums from heavily laden branches. Picking off some of the young fruit helped the remaining fruit to develop into nice-sized produce. Customers who visited the farm's market wanted mature fruit that had received plenty of sunshine and nutrients.

The goal of a fruit farmer is to produce good fruit. The goal of a Christian is also to produce good fruit—spiritual sons and daughters. That is, we want to influence others for Christ so that they turn to Him as Lord. That may happen as we speak of Him. But since actions often speak louder than words, we can also grow spiritual fruit by living lives laced with love, joy, peace, patience, kindness, goodness, faithfulness, gentleness, and self-control (see these fruit of the Spirit in Galatians 5:22, 23). Such qualities attract people hungry for fruit.

In the natural world, good fruit provides the vitamins and minerals we need to develop healthy bodies. On our spiritual journey, good fruit—the effect of our works done in the power of the Spirit—inspires others to come to Christ.

Dear Lord, fill me with the fruit of Your Spirit so that I may pass it on to others in word and in deed. May my life be transformed by Your presence so that others may come to know You. In Jesus' name, amen.

Drop That Anchor!

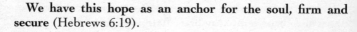

We have this hope as an anchor for the soul, firm and secure (Hebrews 6:19).

Scripture: Hebrews 6:13-20
Song: "I Would Be True"

Early martyrs amaze me. Vibia Perpetua nursed an infant when arrested after Roman emperor Septimius Severus declared it illegal to speak of Christianity. Her father begged her to recant her faith, but she stood firm. Her pregnant slave, Felicitas, was also arrested. The women prayed that she would have her baby early so that she might have the privilege of suffering for her faith along with Perpetua in a Roman arena.

To them, Heaven was so real that they considered it a privilege to give their lives for Christ.

Would I do the same? I honestly don't know. I do know that God offers me daily opportunities to strengthen my faith so that it remains firm and secure. By reading Scripture, I learn how God has worked in this world down through history. By praying, I connect with someone who loves me more than I can imagine.

By reading about early Christians and fellowshiping with Christians today, I hear of their faith in trying circumstances and how God ministered to them. I don't want to miss any opportunity for God to strengthen my faith. You see, I want to be ready—no matter what.

Dear Lord, thank You for promising to be with me, no matter what the circumstances. I trust that as trying times come into my life I will have a wonderful sense of Your presence . . . and hold firm to the faith. In Jesus' name, amen.

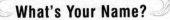

What's Your Name?

The LORD had said to Abram, "Leave your country, your people and your father's household and go to the land I will show you" (Genesis 12:1).

Scripture: Genesis 12:1-9
Song: "Where He Leads Me"

Given the name Isabella at birth, Sojourner Truth, a former slave, changed her name to reflect her calling to ministry. "Sojourner" represented her itinerant lifestyle, and "Truth" described the message of God that she declared. We can imagine the opposition a black woman faced in the mid-1800s as she advocated abolition and women's suffrage across New York, Connecticut, and Massachusetts. Sojourner even took a trip west in response to God's call.

We read in Genesis how another person experienced a name change in response to God's call. Born Abram, which means "exalted father," his name was changed by God to Abraham, which means "father of many." Abraham left his homeland to settle in a foreign country—and became a great nation—simply because God asked him to go.

These individuals offer sterling examples of obedience to the Lord. By prayer, study, and consultation with other Christians, I have also tried to discern God's will for my life. I'm not sure how He might change my name. But I am sure that God is able to use me, and any other person, who says "yes" in response to His call.

Dear Lord, thank You for the promise to go with me wherever You call me to go. Please show me the path You have for my life, step by step. In Jesus' name, amen.

Contentment in a Tent

**By faith he [Abraham] made his home in the promised land
. . . he lived in tents, as did Isaac and Jacob, who were heirs
with him of the same promise** (Hebrews 11:9).

Scripture: Hebrews 11:8-16
Song: "I've Got a Mansion over the Hilltop"

In a grainy black-and-white photo sit three young men warming their hands over a fire. Snow is piled high around them, and a tent sits in the background. Mark and his friends decided to go tent camping one wintry weekend. They toughed it out in freezing temperatures and had a great time. When they followed up that winter adventure with a warmer one in spring, water and mud seeped slowly into their tent. They had little faith they'd be well protected this time. So . . . they headed to a hotel with a solid foundation — and dry bedding.

Contentment in a tent doesn't come easy. But Abraham and his immediate descendants couldn't escape to a hotel when sand storms blew in or thieves approached. Yet Abraham had the faith and foresight to look forward to "the city with foundations, whose architect and builder is God" (v. 10).

God may not call us to pack up and move into a tent as He called Abraham. Yet like Abraham, we too are called to live by faith, to do His bidding, and to content ourselves in His promise of Heaven.

Lord, give me the faith of my spiritual father, Abraham. Teach me to be content wherever You direct me, knowing that You are always with me. Through Christ, amen.

December 5–11. **Katherine Douglas** lives in Swanton, Ohio, where she enjoys writing devotionals for several publications. She's also written a number of devotional books for people with pets.

By Faith, Abraham . . .

By faith Abraham, when God tested him, offered Isaac as a sacrifice (Hebrews 11:17).

Scripture: Hebrews 11:17-22
Song: "Find Us Faithful"

Lloyd Ogilvie, chaplain of the US Senate from 1995 to 2008, once made this observation: "Far too many of us are not attempting anything bold, adventuresome, and courageous enough to need the Spirit's wisdom and power, much less His fire." What an indictment of my own paltry faith.

Over a dozen times in Hebrews 11, we find the phrase "by faith." In today's verses we're told of the faith of the patriarchs and others. By faith these men and women acted on what they believed and in whom they trusted. What they did, what they said, how they conducted their lives, challenges us to step outside our own daily routines.

What is God calling you to do? Take in an ailing loved one? Work at a soup kitchen? Man a polling place? Help in the church nursery? Participate in a short-term missions trip? Go back to school? Start a Bible study in your neighborhood?

Not everything God calls us to do is big—except, perhaps, to us. We've never done it before, or we don't think we're up to the challenge? That's why we are called to do the best things—not necessarily the biggest things—"by faith."

What will you do by faith today?

Lord, I want to put my faith to work. Make me willing to stretch myself beyond what I think I can do and trust what You can indeed do through me. In the powerful name of Jesus I pray, amen.

Good Credit

So then, he is the father of all who believe but have not been circumcised, in order that righteousness might be credited to them (Romans 4:11).

Scripture: Romans 4:9-15
Song: "Father Abraham"

"Credit debt? Bad credit? No credit at all? We can help!"

Have you heard that advertisement on the radio? If by default, identity theft, or poor money management we've gotten into debt, a number of companies stand ready to help . . . for a price.

When it comes to our debt of sin before a holy God, there's no self-induced bailout plan. No religious ceremony or accomplishment of good works can reverse our bad credit before God. For biblical Abraham and his people, neither could circumcision transform the heart. The only way to have a clear and clean record before God is through faith. In faith we trust God to do what we are powerless to do.

What makes this God-given righteousness even more special is that it's called "blessedness" (v. 9). Blessedness touches all of life. It brings peace, joy, and assurance. Not even a good credit rating can bring all of that into our lives. Just as we sang the chorus as children in Sunday school, so too again we can declare: "Father Abraham has many sons . . . I am one of them and so are you. So let's all praise the Lord!"

Father, I'm humbled by the righteousness of Christ that You give me through faith. I know that everything that I have is a gift from You. Thank You for the blessedness You bring into my life. Through Christ I pray. Amen.

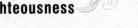

Alien Righteousness

Also for us, to whom God will credit righteousness — for us who believe in him who raised Jesus our Lord from the dead (Romans 4:24).

Scripture: Romans 4:16-25
Song: "Heaven Came Down and Glory Filled My Soul"

I've sat in the captain's chair. When the Star Trek tour came to Detroit, Michigan, in 2009, I plopped myself down in the captain's chair (wearing my official Star Trek insignia T-shirt), and I looked around the reconstructed *Enterprise* "bridge" from the set of the 1960s television series. What a heady moment! I didn't see, nor did I expect to see, any aliens. I may be a rabid "Trekker," but I don't for a minute believe in Klingons, or Romulans, or even UFOs. I do, however, believe in an alien righteousness.

"Alien righteousness." I first heard that term used by a Sunday school teacher. He was teaching on the passage we read today in Romans 4. Righteousness, provided for us by God himself through the atoning work of Jesus Christ, is imputed — *credited* — to our account — by the grace of God.

God's righteousness is alien in that it is something outside us. It comes from beyond us. We can't manufacture it, work ourselves into it, or obtain it by any means. We are incapable of righteousness apart from its gift by the Creator of time and space.

Righteous God, I know I have no righteousness in myself, though I want to live righteously. Live in and through me, Lord Jesus, by the power of Your Holy Spirit. I pray in Your precious name. Amen.

A Covenant Remembered

He remembers his covenant forever, the word he commanded, for a thousand generations, the covenant he made with Abraham, the oath he swore to Isaac (Psalm 105:8, 9).

Scripture: Psalm 105:4-11
Song: "Fear Not, Thou Faithful Christian Flock"

When the League of Nations formed after World War I, its Covenant included a five-point pledge. Number one on the list stated that member nations would protect "the territorial integrity of other member states." Even though U.S. President Woodrow Wilson spearheaded the formation of the League of Nations and its Covenant, the U.S. as a whole wanted nothing to do with it. The United States adopted an isolationist policy. In less than a generation, the League quickly unraveled. Its Covenant was of no effect when World War II erupted.

The Bible abounds with covenants. God's covenant with humankind through Noah (Genesis 9:8-17), God's covenant with Israel through Abraham (numerous texts, including today's), God's covenant through the Law, and finally, God's "better covenant" with us through Christ Jesus (see Hebrews 7–13).

When God makes a covenant, He can and will fulfill it. What He promised to Abraham, He reiterated to Isaac and repeated to Jacob. And, indeed, the Israelites eventually returned to their covenant land. Yes, when He establishes a covenant, God sees it through—everlastingly.

I thank You, **Lord,** that Your covenants are true and eternally binding. Thank You that what You promise You see through to completion. I praise You, Lord, my covenant-keeping God. In the name of Jesus I pray. Amen.

No Surprises Here

May the God of peace, who through the blood of the eternal covenant brought back from the dead our Lord Jesus, that great Shepherd of the sheep, equip you with everything good for doing his will (Hebrews 13:20, 21).

Scripture: Hebrews 13:17-21
Song: "Worthy the Lamb"

For her 40th birthday, Lois's husband hosted a surprise birthday party. Amazingly, she never even suspected it. Her husband didn't let their kids in on the secret—not even the collegian, who undoubtedly could have kept the surprise a secret. What made it extra special for Lois was the presence of her mom and dad. They made the 600-mile round trip just for her.

No one likes a bad surprise. There's nothing like a good surprise, however, to bring simultaneous laughter, excitement, and tears. To pull off a good surprise brings its challenges, but what a treat for everyone when it happens.

God has never been, nor will He ever be surprised. Before He established time, He knew from eternity that the crown of His creation, mankind, would sin. And He knew what He would do. He planned accordingly and made provision for our salvation "before the foundation of the world" (1 Peter 1:20, *KJV*).

I suspect we may have more than a few surprises awaiting us in Heaven. But as for our God, He is never surprised.

Dear Father, it humbles me to think that You planned for my salvation from eternity. Help me to live thankfully and honorably before You, in my thought life and in everything I do and say. Thank You for the shed blood of Jesus on my behalf. In the name of the Father, the Son, and the Holy Spirit, I pray. Amen.

Cutting Covenant

When the sun had set and darkness had fallen, a smoking firepot with a blazing torch appeared and passed between the pieces (Genesis 15:17).

Scripture: Genesis 15:1-6, 12-18
Song: "Nothing but the Blood"

The year was 1960, and two preteen girls took a break from their play. Linda pulled a safety pin out of her pocket. "We can seal our friendship forever by becoming blood sisters."

Susan regarded her friend warily. "How do we become 'blood sisters'?"

"We just prick our fingers with this pin, then put them together to mix our blood. Ta-da! Blood sisters! Want to?"

Squeamish Susan opted out. "Nah. We'll always be best friends anyway."

This (thankfully, no-longer popular) childhood ritual probably came from the practice of "cutting covenant." In the classic work, *The Blood Covenant,* by H. Clay Trumbull, the author describes variations of blood covenant in ancient cultures the world over.

God, the initiator of covenant, established His covenant with Abraham by and through blood. Today's lesson takes us to the covenantal event we've studied all week. Pointing to the stars, God tells Abraham that His covenant with him reaches much further than the patriarch can imagine. Yet, through faith like Abraham's, we're blessed by the new covenant made in Christ.

I praise You, **Father.** You keep every covenant and every promise You make. I pray that I never make a promise I can't or don't intend to keep. In Christ's name, amen.

Abundant Provisions

My God will meet all your needs according to His glorious riches in Christ Jesus (Philippians 4:19).

Scripture: Philippians 4:15-20
Song: "God Will Take Care of You"

We were strangers in a strange land. Twenty of us arrived in palm tree–dotted Costa Rica for a few adventures—and to do volunteer work in small highland villages. Half our group spoke Spanish, and the other half relied on crinkled cheat sheets.

But our three guides set us at ease instantly when they introduced themselves in English and helped load our luggage onto the bus. Within minutes, they gave each of us a personalized handbook, outlining each day's itinerary. The book also contained useful Spanish phrases, local expressions, food recommendations, currency conversion charts, and a set of Costa Rican–themed crossword puzzles to play while traveling.

Our guides not only met our needs, but also exceeded our expectations. They anticipated our uneasiness in a new culture and addressed that anxiety. On the fourth day of our stay, a squirrel monkey bit one of our students. Our guides called the home office and then drove us to a hospital.

On a much larger scale, God does something similar. From the wealth of His riches and His knowledge of eternity, He amply provides for our every need.

Father, thank You for demonstrating Your loving care by often providing for me before I even realize my needs exist. In Jesus' name, amen.

December 12–18. **Vicki Hodges** lives in the mountains of western Colorado, where she's a Spanish teacher at one of the local high schools.

Extraordinary Living

His son by the slave woman was born in the ordinary way; but his son by the free woman was born as the result of a promise (Galatians 4:23).

Scripture: Galatians 4:21-28
Song: "Rejoice in the Lord"

Food? Check. Sleeping bags? Check. Matches? Check. Our family intended to camp in a remote mountain range of western Colorado. We wouldn't see other people for several days.

Autumn rainstorms saturated the ground, and nighttime temperatures hovered around freezing. When we finally located a campsite and pulled in, our pickup and trailer were mired in the mud. We unhitched the trailer, shoveled, pried, pushed, and pulled, but we were hopelessly stuck. As angry storm clouds gathered overhead, we asked God for help.

Nothing happened: no superhuman strength, no bursts of extreme adrenaline, no helicopter. Finally, we decided to ride the four-wheel ATV off the mountain and travel toward the nearest town to contact a towing company. But after driving five miles, we met two guys in a heavy-duty pickup. Within an hour, they had winched us free of the swampy muck.

Abraham and Sarah had asked God to give them a child and expected Him to fulfill their request in the normal way. When He didn't do it, they abandoned the idea. However, God's plan was to operate through the modality of impossibility. He chose to delight them with the extraordinary.

Lord, remind me that whether You answer my prayers in an astonishing manner or without flair, Your ways are always good. Through Christ, amen.

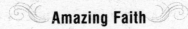

Amazing Faith

I will surely bless you and make your descendants as numerous as the stars in the sky and as the sand on the seashore. Your descendants will take possession of the cities of their enemies (Genesis 22:17).

Scripture: Genesis 22:15-19
Song: "Faith Is the Victory!"

"I was really nervous because I've never done this before. And I think Indy was nervous too. She kept shaking because there were flies, so I held on really tight—I didn't want to fall off. But I believed that Indy wouldn't let me fall. I just knew she wouldn't because I know she believes in me as much as I believe in her." These were William Sylvester's thoughts, as quoted in the *Tribune & Georgian* newspaper in Camden County, Georgia. William is a 12-year-old with autism. At the Special Olympics state horse show, he and Indy, his favorite quarter horse, made a great team. And this young boy's faith in his horse was rewarded with a first place medal.

God honored Abraham's amazing faith and obedience by promising to multiply his descendants beyond numbering. Astronomers believe there are more stars in the universe than grains of sand on the earth. God has most assuredly fulfilled His promise to Abraham; his descendants are countless down through the ages.

Lord, thank You that through faith I can become more than a medal-winning conqueror through Christ. When I'm nervous and uncertain about situations in life, help me have the confidence to approach You with solid faith. I trust You to be faithful to Your promises to provide for me and to protect me. In Jesus' name, amen.

A Remarkable Gift

If one of you says to him, "Go, I wish you well; keep warm and well fed," but does nothing about his physical needs, what good is it? (James 2:16).

Scripture: James 2:14-24
Song: "My Life Is in You, Lord"

"I cleaned out my closet and found some black dress shoes for you, Aimee. You can try them on at church tonight." Linda arrived with three trash bags of shoes for our daughter. Annoyed that she had to rummage through 31 pairs of unwanted castoffs, Aimee searched for the ebony shoes and jammed the bags into the trunk of our car. As she entered church more than slightly frustrated, she observed that one of the usually hyperactive teenage girls was barefoot and uncharacteristically solemn.

"Krista, why aren't you wearing shoes on such a freezing, snowy night?" Krista explained that because they had left home in a hurry she forgot her shoes and her dad refused to return home in order to retrieve them. Aimee immediately felt remorse for being aggravated and asked Krista to select a pair of shoes from the "shoe closet" in our crowded trunk. God had answered Krista's unsolicited request before she even voiced a need.

Aimee could have chosen to scold or tease Krista for forgetting her shoes. Or she could have told Krista she hoped she would be warm enough in bare feet. Yet the truth of one of our favorite quotes rang clear. "Your walk talks, and your talk talks, but your walk talks louder than your talk talks."

Lord, remind me to live the gospel and not just talk about it. Help me turn personal frustration into blessings for others. In Christ's name, amen.

Talking Rocks

If they ever say this to us, or to our descendants, we will answer: Look at the replica of the LORD's altar, which our fathers built, not for burnt offerings and sacrifices, but as a witness between us and you (Joshua 22:28).

Scripture: Joshua 22:21-29
Song: "When I Look into Your Holiness"

"How much farther? We've been driving forever. There's nothing to do, and we're hungry." The highway between Rock Springs and Jackson Hole, Wyoming, consists of beautiful scenery, but also stretches of dry barrenness. My husband invented the car game, "Who can find the most antelope along the side of the road while we're driving to Yellowstone National Park?" The kids entertained themselves for at least an hour by scouring the hillsides in order to locate antelope. Steve promised to award the winner with a candy bar.

Somewhere between the 13th and 17th antelope, our daughter, Marci, began noticing waist-high stacks of rocks on the hillsides. She asked Steve if he could explain them. He said that sometimes sheepherders built monuments from rocks in order to mark the location of nearby water holes. Sometimes the monuments commemorated a notable grave site.

People saw the altar that the children of Reuben and Gad had built. They, like Marci, wondered about stacked stones. They eventually realized it was never used for sacrifice. The memorial spoke of a close association with each other and with the Lord.

Father, thank You for making Christ the great altar, bridging the way of communion between You and me. In Your holy name I pray, amen.

Heed the Warnings!

Every way of a man is right in his own eyes: but the LORD pondereth the hearts. An high look, and a proud heart, and the plowing of the wicked, is sin (Proverbs 21:2, *King James Version*).

Scripture: Proverbs 21:1-5
Song: "Be Still for the Presence"

"Warning: Vaporizer produces hot steam and could cause injuries." Similar warning signs infiltrate our society. Toy labels warn of the choking hazard of small pieces, road signs warn of dangerous curves, and weather channels warn of upcoming storms. Sleeping pills even warn of the possibility . . . that they may cause drowsiness!

With such warnings so common, it's curious that we would ever choose to do wrong. Our friend, Tom, recently made poor choices in his relationship with his girlfriend. Several people advised him to end the relationship and warned him about her behavior. Nevertheless, he ignored us all and did what he thought was right. Months later, he learned his girlfriend had deceived him, dated other guys while they were engaged, and plunged him into significant debt.

How often do I ignore warnings and consequently yield to sin? God's Word abounds in gentle (and not-so-gentle) warnings. Any of us would be wise to pay careful attention. Every one of those warnings is for our own good.

Father, You will never lead me in the wrong direction. Your wisdom has my best always in mind. So please remind me never to settle for less than what You intend for me and help me be wise enough to heed life's warnings. In Jesus' name, amen.

He Did the Unthinkable

When they reached the place God had told him about, Abraham built an altar there and arranged the wood on it. He bound his son Isaac and laid him on the altar, on top of the wood (Genesis 22:9).

Scripture: Genesis 22:1-14
Song: "O How Happy Are They Who the Savior Obey"

As winter settles in, an unthinkable process transpires: the wood frog (*Rana sylvatica*) becomes . . . a frogsicle! Yes, wood frogs can tolerate freezing. In fact, they freeze and defrost with their surroundings. When water in the environment becomes frozen, up to two-thirds of the frog's bodily fluids freeze. Normally, ice in body tissues is lethal. So what enables a wood frog to "die" and come back to life without experiencing these problems?

Its liver produces glucose, a form of sugar, which acts as an antifreeze. This thick syrup protects vital organs while the frog is frozen. When the frogsicle thaws, it does the unthinkable. It immediately begins breathing, its heart beats again, and it returns to normal living.

Abraham could have headed in the opposite direction from where God directed. He might have chosen to sacrifice an animal. He could have refused to submit to God at all. However, Abraham's love for God, complete trust in Him, and unwavering obedience enabled him to do the unthinkable: prepare to sacrifice his son on the altar.

Lord, help me obey You, led by Your Word and the good guidance of others in Your church. Give me a deep passion for submission to Your will. In Jesus' name, amen.

❧ I Am His! ☙

He anointed us, set his seal of ownership on us, and put his Spirit in our hearts as a deposit, guaranteeing what is to come (2 Corinthians 1:21, 22).

Scripture: 2 Corinthians 1:18-22
Song: "O Love That Wilt Not Let Me Go"

My husband and I looked at many houses when we were downsizing. After awhile, they all began to look the same. We waffled in our decision making. By the time we expressed interest in making an offer, the homes we considered were sold. Someone else saw the value in the home before we did.

Then one day our realtor gave us a peek at a home that had just hit the market. "It's a fixer-upper that might meet your needs." And indeed it did. Many projects lay ahead for us with this home, but we could also see its wonderful potential. With labor and love, this house could truly become our home. We didn't want to let this one go.

So we made an offer on the spot. When the realtor told us she would need a deposit, we didn't hesitate to write a check. We wanted this house. That deposit guaranteed our good faith with the mortgage company, and in due time, the house became ours.

Similarly, Jesus will not let us go. He paid for us with His precious blood. The Spirit He placed within us, His deposit toward our final redemption, will help us to find His purpose in our lives.

O Great King, thank You for Your sacrifice on the cross. You paid the ultimate price for me, and I want so much to become the person that you see, hidden within. Thank You for valuing me so highly. In Your precious name I pray. Amen.

Here He Comes!

You saw the suffering of our forefathers in Egypt; you heard their cry at the Red Sea (Nehemiah 9:9).

Scripture: Nehemiah 9:6-10
Song: "Leaning On the Everlasting Arms"

Jamie looked out the window and dabbed at stinging tears. Since learning of her son's terminal diagnosis, her life abruptly changed. Now she needed to learn nursing skills in order to care for him in their home. And ultimately, she had to prepare for the day her child would go to Heaven. Overwhelmed, the young woman cried out to God for help. Did He even hear her?

The Israelites felt overwhelmed and frightened as they faced the Red Sea with Pharaoh's angry army hot on their heels. Imagine their terror, looking out at a billowing sea, hearing the clatter of horse's hooves approaching. They had nowhere to turn.

So they turned to God and cried out to Him, "Help us!" The Lord heard and delivered them in a miraculous way. With a wave of His hand, God parted the waters of the Red Sea and led them across dry land. Then He shut the waters back up, so that the Egyptians could not chase them any further.

Are you in distress? God surely hears your cries. He attended to Jamie's needs and helped her, day by day, to face great difficulty. He hears and remains present with His children through all things.

Heavenly Father, I need Your guidance! Help me to walk faithfully with You and to turn to You in my distress, as my forefathers did. Through Christ, amen.

December 20–25. **Barbara Tuttle** is a freelance writer who contributes to several Christian publications. She and her husband enjoy hiking and cross-country skiing throughout Michigan.

Our Song of Faith

Clearly no one is justified before God by the law, because "The righteous will live by faith" (Galatians 3:11).

Scripture: Galatians 3:6-12
Song: "Falter Not"

"No Admittance." To the small boy who could not yet read, the words on a sign that hung above the concert hall door meant nothing. While his mother chatted away with friends and waited for the concert to begin, the bored child simply wandered off. Now he stood alone in the private section reserved for musicians. Upon opening the door, he saw a magnificent piano. Enthralled, the boy sat down and studiously began to plunk out a little tune.

Imagine his mother's surprise when the curtains suddenly opened, and there sat her son—at the master's piano! Suddenly, Paderewski walked onto the stage. Stretching his arms around the boy, he composed a harmonious accompaniment for the child as he plinked away.

The unsuspecting child in this popular story could not read or follow, the "No Admittance" sign. But the audience delighted to see how the accomplished musician affectionately embraced the child and his song. We too are surrounded by many, many instructions and admonitions in the Scriptures. No one could follow all that it requires of us. But with childlike wonder, we can play our song of faith for Jesus, and He will accept us.

Dear God, I cannot begin to keep the requirements of your holy law. It seems the more I try to do everything right, the more I fail. You are a just and Holy God, and I thank You for sending Jesus to accomplish salvation for me. In His name, amen.

A Sure Foundation

Brothers, let me take an example from everyday life. Just as no one can set aside or add to a human covenant that has been duly established, so it is in this case (Galatians 3:15).

Scripture: Galatians 3:13-18
Song: "Father, Whose Everlasting Love"

"I do." Many a jittery bride and groom can attest to a case of nerves when speaking their wedding vows. Marriage is an honorable, sacred covenant, and it's natural to tremble at the altar.

Yet in many cultures, the marriage union begins the moment promises are conferred, before the actual ceremony to seal the vows. When a man proposes to his beloved, he makes a promise, and she eagerly accepts.

Sometimes, families of the prospective bride and groom arrange the marriage. They may barely know each other, but the promise is conferred. These individual and collective promises are generally recognized by a period of engagement, or betrothal, before the ceremony. The promises made in our hearts and affirmed in community then enable us to live out our marriage vows. We rest in the promise of loyalty to one another, no matter what trials may come.

Many years ago, God promised blessings to Abraham and his seed. It was an honorable, sacred covenant. And down through time, the promise has not been set aside. Through faith in Jesus Christ, it continues now to all who believe!

Gracious Father, thank You for the covenant You have made with me through Your Son, Jesus. Teach me to have respect for promises. I don't want to make promises to others carelessly; I need Your help to keep them. In Jesus' name, amen.

One Heart, One Will

"I am the Lord's servant," Mary answered. "May it be to me as you have said." Then the angel left her (Luke 1:38).

Scripture: Luke 1:26-38
Song: "Ye Servants of God"

"I knew what I was getting into when my husband enlisted in the army. I anticipated long deployments overseas. But I love my husband, and I'm committed to our marriage, so I simply adjust to his absence in our home."

The young woman bravely faced interviewers recently on a television show depicting the lives of military families. Surely she carried a heavy load, managing the countless details of running a household and parenting alone. But she willingly learned new skills and embraced self-reliance.

Her young soldier in the field must have felt blessed to have a faithful wife taking good care of his family. He knew that she understood his job and respected his duty to their country. For his sake, she put her fears aside and tackled each new challenge with a can-do spirit.

Because she aligned her heart with her husband's, this military wife possessed the grace of acceptance. Military families endure unique hardships willingly. They faithfully follow their commander-in-chief.

Am I following my commander-in-chief? Are my heart and will aligned with God's?

Dear Lord, cultivate in me a willing heart and spirit to do Your will. Sometimes I resist doing the hard things, and often I fear the unknown. But I do want to wholeheartedly embrace the adventure of serving You. Through Christ I pray. Amen.

Leap, O Spirit!

When Elizabeth heard Mary's greeting, the baby leaped in her womb, and Elizabeth was filled with the Holy Spirit (Luke 1:41).

Scripture: Luke 1:39-45
Song: "Mary's Boy Child"

John the Baptist, the child Elizabeth carried in her womb, would grow up to preach a baptism of repentance for the forgiveness of sins. But John had no authority to forgive. He preached and baptized to point people to Jesus, the Messiah, who alone could forgive sins.

Even as a baby in his mother's womb, John's spirit recognized the Holy One inside Mary's womb. No wonder he leapt with joy! John would spend his life preparing the people's hearts for Jesus and His righteous message.

The authority of Jesus continues to bring people under conviction for their sins. Many worshipers "grip the pew" in front of them when God's Word pricks their heart and conscience. I've been there. And I am thankful when Jesus convicts me of sin. After all, I know that I can confess my sins and be forgiven.

Oh, that our spirits too would leap within us when we sense the presence of our Lord!

Almighty and most merciful God, teach me to worship You with great joy. Help me to recognize greatness each time that I hear Your name. May I honor You in all I do, and may my spirit leap within me each time I hear of the great things You have done. Give me the courage to speak of Your greatness to others. In the name of Jesus I pray. Amen.

∼ **Make Room for Jesus** ∼

She gave birth to her firstborn, a son. She wrapped him in cloths and placed him in a manger, because there was no room for them in the inn (Luke 2:7).

Scripture: Luke 1:46-55; 2:1-7
Song: "My Heart, Your Home"

We recently downsized into a smaller home. Of course, this meant we had to part with many of our belongings. Everything in the old household received a questioning look: *Do we really need that?* We scrutinized our closets, kitchen cabinets, and furnishings. We hauled numerous dusty things from the basement and attacked the clutter in our garage. We even repeated this process several times, constantly confronting our emotional attachments to familiar things around us.

As we whittled away at our belongings, finding things to donate, locating people with needs, the process grew easier. One thought guided our choices: What do we want to make room for in our new, smaller house? We wanted our home to be a peaceful place and a soft place to land at the end of a long working day. We also wanted it to be a welcoming place for family and friends.

Because there was no room for Him in the inn, Jesus was born in a manger. Perhaps the cluttered state of our home in some way reflects our heart. As I look around today, I am asking, have I made room for Jesus in my home and in my heart?

O Lord, I want my heart to be a welcoming place for You. I pray that You will show me anything there that blocks communion with You. Please prick my conscience when I allow any manner of ungodliness to creep in. I love You. Through Christ, amen.

God Is Already There

He called down famine on the land and destroyed all their supplies of food; and He sent a man before them — Joseph, sold as a slave (Psalm 105:16, 17).

Scripture: Psalm 105:16-22
Song: "Do I Trust You?"

"How could this be part of God's plan for my life?" my 16-year-old daughter, Sarah, asked. My recent cancer diagnosis had shaken her faith.

I wondered about this too but I said, "God has a plan for our good and His glory. He knows the future. He is already there."

Sarah could not see past her concern. Fears of the future loomed with menace. What if her mother died? How could God allow this?

Sarah didn't yet know that her experience could serve to comfort others or that it would draw her nearer to the heart of God in ways that nothing else would. Five years later, God called Sarah to minister to orphans in Kenya.

Similarly, Joseph must have wondered how being sold into slavery by his brothers could possibly be God's plan. With a broken heart and his feet in fetters, could Joseph even imagine that he would one day rule over the king's house? Yet God sent Joseph ahead to prepare for the future during a time of famine. Whatever the future holds, God is already there.

Eternal God, You hem me in with Your love. All the days ordained for me were planned before one of them came to be. Thank You! In Christ's holy name, amen.

December 26-31. **Julie Kloster** is a freelance writer, speaker, and teacher living in Sycamore, Illinois, with her husband and three daughters.

God Is with Me

Because the patriarchs were jealous of Joseph, they sold him as a slave into Egypt. But God was with him and rescued him from all his troubles (Acts 7:9, 10).

Scripture: Acts 7:9-16
Song: "God Is with Me"

"This will probably be the most difficult classroom you will ever experience," the administrator told me during the interview. Her message left me with some fears. But she couldn't dissuade me from the task at hand. After being a stay-at-home mom for 20 years, God was leading me back to teach in the public schools.

The first few months were a daily battle for the hearts and souls of these scarred and hurting children. Autism, bipolar disorder, emotional disturbance, and oppositional-defiance disorder accounted for their struggles. God reminded me that His mercies were new every morning, and in the evenings He reminded me that He had been faithful and ever-present. And eventually I gained the goodwill of my students and faculty.

This same God was also with Joseph thousands of years before I was born. Though Joseph was sold into slavery, God was with him and gave him wisdom. This young man eventually gained the goodwill of Pharaoh who made him ruler of Egypt. In that position Joseph provided for the very ones who had sold him into slavery. God rescued Joseph from his troubles and gave him the grace to forgive.

God, even on days when I feel I can't go on, Your compassion sustains me. Though I walk in the midst of trouble, You are with me. Thank You, in Jesus' name. Amen.

Not My Will

Father, if you are willing, take this cup from me; yet not my will, but yours be done (Luke 22:42).

Scripture: Luke 22:39-46
Song: "I Surrender All"

"Your baby may not live." The doctor's voice was just above a whisper. "Because she's 15 weeks premature, she needs a full respirator and 100% oxygen. We are doing everything we can."

I nodded numbly as my heart cried out to God. "Lord, my God, You know how I love this child. I beg You to heal her." I physically opened my clenched fists to signify the release of my will. Hot tears dripped on my open palms as I prayed, "Lord, You love her more than I do. She is yours. Not my will, but Yours be done."

I learned these words from Jesus, who prayed them fervently in the Garden of Gethsemane. Facing the cross, Jesus struggled in prayer. Praying in the garden with His disciples was Jesus' usual custom, yet this time Jesus told His disciples to pray to fight temptation. Was this the temptation that wants our own will more than God's?

Through fervent prayer God gives us the grace and strength to trust Him. My premature daughter is a musically gifted 16-year-old today. Yet if God had called her home, His character would have stayed the same. He is a God of mercy and kindness who does all things for His glory and our good.

Father, You know how many hairs are on my head, and You are intimately acquainted with all my ways. Please give me the strength and courage to trust Your will, even when I do not understand Your ways. In the precious name of Jesus I pray. Amen.

Warning Examples

These things happened to them as examples and were written down as warnings for us, on whom the fulfillment of the ages has come (1 Corinthians 10:11).

Scripture: 1 Corinthians 10:1-13
Song: "Come, Thou Fount of Every Blessing"

"She doesn't have any food in her house," Sheila said, expressing heartfelt concern. "The minute she gets paid she finds a bar, and then she asks me for money to pay her bills." Sheila had grown up in a single-parent home with her alcoholic mother, and she still dealt with the emotional turmoil.

"I don't know how to help my mom," Sheila explained. "But this I do know—by God's grace, I will *not* continue the typical generational cycle of alcoholism."

Sheila had learned a life lesson from her mother's negative example. In a sense, God used Sheila's childhood pain to warn her, and she allowed God to provide a way through the years ahead. She would not fall into the same temptations with alcohol that had enslaved her mother.

Today's Scripture tells us that the Israelites' choices and behaviors are recorded to warn us. God wants us to understand important lessons from the failings of those who have gone before us. We are all human and easily capable of giving in to temptation. However, thankfully, God is there to help us through every potential hazard.

God, You know my thoughts and motives. Though I love You, I know I am prone to wander. Please forgive me for the many times I have sinned against You, and keep me from temptation in the days ahead. I pray in the name of Jesus. Amen.

Wonder of Wonders

Let me understand the teaching of your precepts; then I will mediate on your wonders (Psalm 119:27).

Scripture: Psalm 119:25-32
Song: "God of Wonders"

In 1943 Dionisio Pulido, a Mexican farmer, began his spring planting. Suddenly, a 150-foot fissure opened in the ground. "I felt a thundering," Pulido explained. "The trees trembled . . . there was a hiss or whistle, loud and continuous; and there was a smell of sulphur." In the middle of Pulido's field, a volcano was born. Over the next few days, the volcano hurled flaming rock bombs more than a thousand feet into the air. Lava buried his cornfields. Pulido and the world watched in wonder.

God reveals himself in the wonders of nature, in the Grand Canyon, Mount Everest, the Northern Lights, and so many other awe-inspiring sites worldwide. Everyday beauties of nature, like the pink, azure, and frosty white sky at sunrise on an icy morning are often just as breathtaking.

Nature causes us to stand in awe of God, yet the psalmist in today's passage speaks of a different kind of wonder — the wonder of meditating on God's Word. Weary and full of sorrow, the psalmist pours out his heart to the Lord. And the Lord listens, answers, strengthens, and sets the psalmist's heart free. Is there any greater wonder than knowing that God speaks to us with the love letter of His Word?

God of Wonders, You are holy. Maker of the universe, please reveal Your heart to me anew every morning. I stand in awe of You, God. The world was formed when You spoke, and You speak to me daily through Your Word. In Jesus' name, amen.

Seeking True Success

The LORD was with Joseph and he prospered, and he lived in the house of his Egyptian master (Genesis 39:2).

Scripture: Genesis 39:1-6
Song: "I'd Rather Have Jesus"

"A kind heart and a good attitude can take you to new heights of success in your personal and professional lives," says Victor Parachin in an article for *Advisor Today*. Parachin suggests that to be successful in business we need to learn from criticism, maintain an upbeat attitude, help our coworkers, and show appreciation.

Finding grains of truth in criticism demonstrates the humility that God calls us to have. And by showing kindness and appreciation, we glorify God, enjoying a success that is eternal not simply temporal.

It is likely that Joseph lived by these principles too, as they flow from the Scriptures. The Bible makes it clear that Joseph was successful in everything he did because God was with him. Sold into servanthood, Joseph quickly became successful and was put in charge of Potiphar's house. (Even Potiphar was blessed by God's faithfulness to Joseph.)

We tend to view success in terms of dollars and cents, don't we? Yet true success can't be measured that way. Even as a servant, we can be successful if we walk with God.

Lord, I'd rather have You in my life than all the riches of the world. Eternal success is found in You alone—in walking close by Your side. When You are with me, I can do all things for You strengthen me. Your ever-present help comforts, consoles, and guides. Please help me to express my gratitude each day. In the name Christ, amen.

DEVOTIONS®

JANUARY

> God is faithful; . . . when you are tempted, he will also provide a way out.
>
> —*1 Corinthians 10:13*

Gary Allen, Editor   **Margaret Williams,** Project Editor   Photo © Liquid Library

❦ I Am Free ❧

While Joseph was there in the prison, the LORD was with him (Genesis 39:20, 21).

Scripture: Genesis 39:7-21
Song: "I Am Free"

"The one thing the DNA revolution has taught us is that there are more innocent people in jail than we ever thought," said Barry Scheck, a law professor at Yeshiva University. Scheck is also the cofounder of the Innocence Project, which has exonerated over 35 inmates using DNA testing. "Any decent person recoils at the horror of an innocent person being put in prison," Scheck said, as he explained his desire to set the innocent free.

Being jailed unjustly is an ancient story. Joseph was falsely accused by Potiphar's wife, so in an angry rage Potiphar confined Joseph to prison. Joseph's desire to obey God and flee temptation was the very thing that led to his imprisonment. Yet God was with Joseph. And no doubt the young man knew that even a whole life in prison with God was better than slavery to the sin that was offered him.

We may not be imprisoned due to false accusations. But to what extent are we chained by our sins and addictions? Wouldn't it be better to have our feet in fetters than our souls enslaved?

O God, the king of glory, in You I have true freedom. You cause darkness to flee and You win the battle for my soul. You paid the price for my freedom at the cross, and You promise to never leave me. Because of You my soul sings, "I am free! Praise God!" I pray this prayer in the name of Jesus, my merciful Savior and Lord. Amen.

January 1. **Julie Kloster** is a freelance writer, speaker, and teacher living in Sycamore, Illinois, with her husband and three daughters.

Opportunities to Minister

When Joseph came to them the next morning, he saw that they were dejected. So he asked Pharaoh's officials . . . "Why are your faces so sad today?" (Genesis 40:6, 7).

Scripture: Genesis 40:1-8
Song: "What a Friend We Have in Jesus"

While her brother rested, Lonora wandered out into the waiting area at Portland VA Medical Center, looking for a quiet place to sort out her thoughts. Anguish filled her heart. Her brother, Ken, lay nearby in the critical care unit. Just weeks before, her other brother had died tragically.

Lonora located a vacant seat and sat down. She needed solitude. Instead, she heard loud, crude remarks being directed at an already distraught woman. Like Lonora, this woman was deeply concerned about a loved one. Comments from insensitive relatives had only made the situation worse. Moved by compassion, Lonora approached her. She spoke words of comfort, offered a short prayer, and then gave her a tender hug. The embrace released tears of healing for both women.

In today's passage Joseph encounters jailed servants who had offended Pharaoh. Thankfully for them, providence had placed Joseph in the same jail to offer encouragement. And God will put needful people in our paths as well. Discouraging circumstances provide the perfect opportunity for ministry.

Spirit of the Living God, many people today face difficulties in their lives. Please lead me to those who need Your encouragement. In Jesus' name I pray. Amen.

January 2–8. **Charles E. Harrel** ministered for more than 30 years before stepping aside to pursue a writing ministry. He enjoys digital photography and playing the 12-string guitar.

A Series of Unfortunate Events

I was forcibly carried off from the land of the Hebrews, and even here I have done nothing to deserve being put in a dungeon (Genesis 40:15).

Scripture: Genesis 40:9-15
Song: "Safely, Safely Gathered In"

The newscast that night caught my attention. A man charged and convicted of a ghastly crime would soon be released from prison. The court system and his attorneys had reopened the case after they discovered certain inconsistencies. After evaluating the new DNA evidence, the jury exonerated him of any crime. Such testing methods were not available during his first trial, so he'd spent 15 years behind bars for a crime he didn't commit. Even so, the man did not appear sad or angry. Instead, he was looking forward to redeeming the time he had lost.

With advances in crime scene investigation, some people wrongly incarcerated are now enjoying freedom, a new lease on life. Joseph found himself in a similar situation. A series of events landed him in an underground prison cell. Yet he had done nothing wrong. Still, he didn't allow his imprisonment to sour his spiritual outlook. He used the situation to tell people about his faith in God.

God often uses adversity to birth a greater purpose for our lives. In Joseph's case, he earned an Egyptian pardon and became Pharaoh's highest-ranking advisor. Exercising patience and trusting God worked for Joseph, and it can for us as well.

O Lord, without all the facts, people are prone to misjudge. When that happens, remind me to pray for wisdom and to trust You for the outcome. Through Christ, amen.

Restoration Still Possible

He restored the chief cupbearer to his position, so that he once again put the cup into Pharaoh's hand (Genesis 40:21).

Scripture: Genesis 40:16-23
Song: "Restore Me"

Paul tiptoed into the house that morning. He didn't want to wake up his wife, not yet anyway, especially with bad news from the workplace. The shift leader at the paper mill had caught Paul sleeping on the job and placed him on temporary leave, pending an investigation.

The 12-hour graveyard shifts at the mill are grueling, and Paul grew tired staring at the pressure gauges at his workstation. He just closed his eyes for a few minutes—right as his supervisor walked by. Paul wasn't the only one that night; the shift leader caught another worker sleeping. The coworker, however, had wandered away from his desk and found a secluded place under a pipe to fall asleep. Luckily, Paul was still sitting at his workstation. After their review, the paper company restored Paul to his position and fired the other guy.

In similar fashion Pharaoh restored the cupbearer to his position while executing the chief baker. (I'm sure the baker disagreed with the decision. No doubt, there were extenuating circumstances.)

God always sees our hearts and knows our true intentions. And like the cupbearer, sometimes we benefit from a season of testing.

Gracious Father, thank You for sending times of testing. Although I don't always understand them, I believe they help me grow stronger. In Jesus' name, amen.

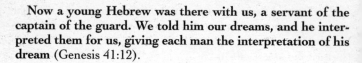

The Correct Interpretation

Now a young Hebrew was there with us, a servant of the captain of the guard. We told him our dreams, and he interpreted them for us, giving each man the interpretation of his dream (Genesis 41:12).

Scripture: Genesis 41:1-13
Song: "The Solid Rock"

I had trouble sleeping that Saturday night. My spirit was troubled—something at the church maybe—I couldn't put my finger on it. Finally, the tiredness overtook me, and I fell into a deep sleep. I usually don't remember my dreams, but this night the dream came alive in vivid detail.

Three lions paced back and forth in the backyard of our parsonage. As they drew closer, I could hear them roaring underneath the bedroom windowsill. Then, I saw three sets of paws tearing at the screen. They were forcing their way into our house, intending to harm my family. I could not let that happen. I jarred myself awake and rushed to the window to face them down. When I got there, I saw nothing.

Unnerved, I sat down and prayed for wisdom. In reply, God gave me a sermon about three problems stalking our church. That Sunday morning, three sin issues were uncovered and dealt with. My dream and its warning proved all too real.

Most dreams are triggered by something we've read, seen on TV, or eaten the night before. Some dreams, however, are God-sent and inspired. I can personally attest to it.

Lord, when I read my Bible, hear a sermon, or study a daily devotional guide, I hear Your gentle voice talking to me. Praise to You, through Christ. Amen.

God Has the Best Answers

"I cannot do it," Joseph replied to Pharaoh, **"but God will give Pharaoh the answer he desires"** (Genesis 41:16).

Scripture: Genesis 41:14-24
Song: "Jesus Is the Answer"

Bob wanted everyone to think he was a prophet. He often told people what God was saying about a certain matter. One Sunday, he decided to comment about the minister's sermon on the benefits of tithing. After waiting for the closing prayer, he stood up and said, "Thus says God . . ." He paused as if the words had just disappeared from his thoughts. So he started again, "Thus says the Lord . . ." Again, he stopped in mid-sentence. After a third attempt with similar results, Bob sat down with this apology: "I really have no idea what God is saying, so please don't listen to me."

In today's passage Pharaoh needed someone to interpret a troubling dream. His wise men and magicians were, like Bob, clueless. When Pharaoh called upon Joseph, he gave the king the true meaning to his dream, but made it clear that the answer came from God.

Likewise, we should seek the Lord for answers—not make up ones that are self-serving or otherwise politically correct. Such responses are often doomed to failure because they are not based on God's plan, nor do they rely on faith. Whether it's a troubling dream, a financial concern, or an unsolvable family problem, we must always ask God for the answer.

Dear Savior, during times of uncertainty, I will wait in prayer until I receive Your reply. Your answer is the only one I truly need. In the name of Jesus I pray. Amen.

The Duplication Factor

The reason the dream was given to Pharaoh in two forms is that the matter has been firmly decided by God, and God will do it soon (Genesis 41:32).

Scripture: Genesis 41:25-36
Song: "Wonderful Words of Life"

After opening our ministerial meeting with prayer, the ministers in Dayton, Oregon, took five minutes to share about last month's ministry. Five ministers were present that day, each one representing a different church denomination. As part of our reports, we shared the title and text of our previous Sunday's sermon. To our amazement, we had all used the same Scripture text, and although our sermon titles were different, the messages we preached were much the same.

As we read our Bibles, we find that certain passages, stories, words, and prophetic dreams are purposely repeated. Many theologians believe something revealed or stated twice in Scripture is God's way of drawing attention to it, like putting an exclamation point at the end of a sentence. The Bible contains numerous examples, including today's passage. Pharaoh's dream came in two forms: seven cows and seven heads of grain. Yet each version held the same warning of an approaching famine.

God still uses repetition to emphasize an important truth. This gives us an opportunity to change our ways and avert a catastrophe. God is merciful and wants us to know His plan for our lives. Besides being expedient, repetition gets our attention.

Father, I appreciate Your loving concern for my soul. Repetition of important truths helps me follow You closer. May I always be attentive. In Jesus' name, amen.

In Whom the Spirit Dwells

Can we find anyone like this man, one in whom is the spirit of God? (Genesis 41:38).

Scripture: Genesis 41:37-46, 50-52
Song: "By My Spirit"

My son, Christopher, grew sicker by the hour. I decided to skip the last service of our citywide crusade at the Portland Coliseum, even though I held a reserved seat with the evangelist on the platform. My wife drove the fully loaded church van in my stead. After the group left, I felt sad, then desperate when I checked my son's temperature: 101 degrees and rising. I strapped him into the car seat and headed to the store for a bottle of children's aspirin.

At the store my line stalled as a couple counted out quarters to buy a handful of groceries. Obviously, they were experiencing hard times. The Holy Spirit tugged at my heart, so I offered to pay for their purchase. He stood speechless; she wept. Now realizing the Spirit had led me there, I shared God's plan of salvation.

When we returned home, I rechecked Christopher's temperature—no fever, no flu symptoms either. That day was providential. For me, ministering to a needy couple proved a higher priority than sitting on the platform with a famous evangelist. When we follow the Holy Spirit's gentle guidance, miracles can happen—and people will find eternal life.

Dear Spirit of God, Your indwelling has many purposes. You lead me each day and help me reach out to others in need. Thank You, Holy Spirit, for giving me wisdom, anointing, and discernment to carry out Your ministry. In Jesus' name, amen.

Feast or Famine

For the famine was in the land of Canaan also (Genesis 42:5).

Scripture: Genesis 42:1-5
Song: "Father, Who Dost Thy Children Feed"

When you hear the expression, "It's either feast or famine," it's usually from someone shocked to find themselves in the midst of a "famine." We tend to take our "feasts" for granted. During times of good health, secure job, enough money, and plenty of food, it's easy to think we must have done something to deserve all the good fortune—and that good times will go on forever.

The people in Genesis 42 enjoyed seven years of literal feast, of great plenty, of record harvests. Then Joseph correctly interpreted Pharaoh's dream and warned him that those seven good years would be followed by seven years of famine, not only in Egypt but throughout the world.

Where are you these days: in feast or famine? good times or bad? Joseph advised Pharaoh to set aside immense stores of grain during the good times so there would be food available during the famine. That advice saved Egypt and the world.

How wise to store up our spiritual resources—our ability to walk close to God—during the good times so we can weather the inevitable bad times. Do you pray and study the Bible daily, storing up wisdom you'll need to survive the next crisis?

O Lord, help me store Your Word in my heart and mind so I always have enough for my needs and for the needs of others. In the precious name of Jesus I pray. Amen.

January 9–15. **Maria Tolar** is a freelance writer living in Portland, Oregon, with her husband. She's an avid member of her church's Bible study group and is currently writing a historical novel.

A Spirit of Excellence

Your servants were twelve brothers, the sons of one man, who lives in the land of Canaan. The youngest is now with our father, and one is no more (Genesis 42:13).

Scripture: 42:6-17
Song: "Lead Me Gently Home, Father"

In a span of just over 20 years, Joseph has moved from his place as his father's favorite son to being a slave. He's been falsely accused by his Egyptian employer's lying wife and thrown into prison. He's accurately interpreted the dreams of fellow prisoners, which leads to one man's release. Two long years later, Pharaoh has a dream no one can decipher. Only then does this fellow remember Joseph, who waits patiently in prison.

Joseph experiences an astounding reversal of fortune. He interprets Pharaoh's puzzling dream, suggests the solution to the dilemma the dream poses, and receives Pharaoh's promotion to overseer of all the land.

But what fascinates us more than these dramatic events in Joseph's life is the character of Joseph. Here is a man of integrity and honor, one without bitterness or malice. He's forgiven his brothers. He's remained close to God. He's so capable and trustworthy that the warden lets Joseph run the jail.

We read of other great men of God in the Old Testament. But many had serious weaknesses and character flaws. Not Joseph. He is one of the marvels of the Old Testament.

Almighty God, may I have an excellent, uncomplaining spirit as Joseph did, keeping my eyes fixed on You, Lord, knowing You have a good plan for my life. In the name of Jesus, who lives and reigns with You and the Holy Spirit. Amen.

Sowing and Reaping

Surely we are being punished because of our brother. We saw how distressed he was when he pleaded with us for his life, but we would not listen; that's why this distress has come upon us (Genesis 42:21).

Scripture: Genesis 42:18-25
Song: "Gathering out of Tears"

Joseph was often sinned against without sinning himself. He was tried repeatedly in his life—and he passed every test. God was with him, blessing him even in prison, preparing Joseph for a great mission.

And then there are Joseph's 10 older brothers, back in Canaan. Consumed by jealously, Joseph's brothers resented his very existence. He was their father's favorite, Scripture says, and they "could not say a kind word about him." Soon, their hatred led to a plot to kill him. When a caravan bound for Egypt crossed their paths, they sold young Joseph into slavery.

Then they went home and lied to their brokenhearted father about Joseph's disappearance. Jacob thought wild animals must have killed his son. Ironically, Jacob had practiced deception against his own father, Isaac. What a family in misery!

Joseph had long since forgiven his brothers. But his brothers never forgave themselves—or each other. For more than 20 years, their own shame and guilt imprisoned them. And their father's continuous grief for his lost son, Joseph, reminded them daily of what they had done.

Dear Lord, I don't want to sow the wind and reap the whirlwind. Examine me and know my thoughts, lest I follow any path that grieves You. Through Christ, amen.

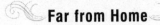
Far from Home

"Is your father still living?" he asked us. **"Do you have another brother?"** (Genesis 43:7).

Scripture: Genesis 43:1-14
Song: "Blest Be the Tie That Binds"

When my husband was a boy, he suffered a serious injury to his eye. He was sent 200 miles from home for expert medical treatment. What he remembers most vividly is not the fear or the pain, but being desperately homesick the entire time he was away from home.

Joseph was an adolescent when he was sold into bondage. He was 20 years older, and the governor of Egypt, when his brothers journeyed there to purchase grain because of a great famine. They bowed down before the most important man in Egypt, not recognizing their little brother. But Joseph recognized them instantly.

If Joseph had been a lesser man, he could have avenged himself on these cruel brothers. He could have gloated at the power he now wielded. Now his brothers were at his mercy!

Instead, he struggled to keep his composure, turning aside to weep. All of the years of being an alien in a strange land overwhelmed him. Though he'd reached the pinnacle of authority and power in Egypt, he was still a devoted son and loyal brother.

How he had longed for home, for his father and his family! Now only compassion filled his heart.

Almighty and merciful God, may I have a tender heart, eager to forgive and forget old wrongs, as You have done for me. In the name of the Father, the Son, and the Holy Spirit, I pray. Amen.

Persecution

Why have you repaid good with evil? (Genesis 44:4)

Scripture: Genesis 44:1-13
Song: "I Would Be True"

In this question, we see the story of mankind—beginning in the Garden of Eden. God created Adam and Eve, and placed them in Paradise, where they made friends with the serpent. That pattern of repaying God's goodness with mankind's evil runs throughout Scripture. Prophets sent to warn God's people are routinely slaughtered by the very people they sought to help.

Joseph's ill treatment by his brothers may shock us, but it is nothing compared to the violence done to believers throughout the ages. Many of the early Christians were martyred for preaching the good news. Persecution of Christians has been a constant throughout history and still continues unabated to this day.

Knowing all this, it's amazing how crushed we can be when we're hurt by people we thought were friends or vilified by people we wanted to help. Recently I heard a minister on the radio explaining the tender way he counsels church members who come to him, weeping about being repaid evil for good.

"I'm shocked that you're shocked," he tells them, "surprised that you're surprised!" Instead of weeping, he tells them, we can rejoice, remembering what the Lord taught: "Blessed are those who are persecuted because of righteousness, for theirs is the kingdom of heaven" (Matthew 5:10).

Lord, let me fight the good fight of faith, even with hurt feelings and bruised ego, as I remember those suffering significant persecution. In Jesus' name, amen.

Redemption

No! Do not let me see the misery that would come upon my father (Genesis 44:34).

Scripture: Genesis 44:24-34
Song: "My Redeemer Lives"

Judah was one of Joseph's older brothers. In later years, Judah received the patriarchal blessing—a great honor since this is the lineage of the Messiah.

When the governor of Egypt (Joseph, whom none of the brothers recognize) decrees that Benjamin must remain behind for stealing a goblet, Judah steps forward.

Judah has been as guilty as any of the brothers in wronging Joseph. But from his words it is clear that in the years since selling his brother into slavery, he has learned a bitter lesson. His father's unrelenting grief over Joseph has tormented Judah. Now if his father loses Benjamin, Judah knows it would "bring the gray head of our father down to the grave in sorrow" (v. 31).

Judah doesn't merely deliver a speech. He proves how sorry he is for what he did over 20 years earlier to Joseph. He now offers to serve as ransom for Benjamin—his life for his brother's. He begs to be imprisoned and serve as a slave for the governor of Egypt.

But let Benjamin go! Their father could bear the loss of Judah, but not of Benjamin. And Judah is willing to suffer the loss of his freedom rather than see his father grieve again. I can learn from this apparent reformation of Judah's heart. Can you?

Praise You, **O Lord,** for sending Your only Son to redeem us and save us—and to wipe away every tear. In His precious name I pray. Amen.

A Purpose-Driven Life

So then, it was not you who sent me here, but God (Genesis 45:8).

Scripture: Genesis 45:3-15
Song: "Lord, Through All the Generations"

When did Joseph realize the truth of verse 8? Did he immediately discern God's great purpose in mind for him, even as the caravan rumbled along, taking him to Egypt to serve as a slave?

Did he realize God had sent him to Egypt for a great purpose when he was unjustly thrown into jail? When he saw God's favor and blessing on his life, even though he remained in prison? Was Joseph's faith in God such that he never stopped expecting blessing from God, no matter the circumstances? Could he see through the present into the future, not only when interpreting dreams but as he examined his own life?

Or did he fully realize God's purpose and perfect timing only when Pharaoh turned over to him the responsibility of running Egypt? I think it was then that it dawned on Joseph, that all his trials had prepared him to be entrusted with the responsibility of saving the world from famine.

But when do we realize that what seems like a catastrophe may well turn out to be a great blessing? May we all be able to someday look back and say, "In all things God works for the good of those who love him, who have been called according to His purpose" (Romans 8:28).

Dearest Lord, You are my shepherd both in green pastures and in the presence of my enemies. My greatest trials bring my greatest blessings when I keep trusting You. Thank You for all Your care down through the years. In Christ's name, amen.

Beginning the Journey

Do not be afraid to go down to Egypt, for I will make you into a great nation there. I will go down to Egypt with you (Genesis 46:3, 4).

Scripture: Genesis 46:1-7
Song: "All the Way My Savior Leads Me"

I found a dime as I walked along the street. I picked it up and slipped it into my pocket. A few yards away something else glinted in the bright sunlight. I detoured to look. It was only the pull-tab from a soft drink can. Several steps farther, a foil gum wrapper glistened like silver.

In those few steps I'd seen a lot of litter and developed a crick in my neck from staring at the ground. About the only thing I learned was that there were no more coins on the pavement.

So I raised my eyes and looked for different things. As I moved on, I discovered a rosebush with beautiful pink blossoms. I spotted a nuthatch spiraling down a tree. I saw the sunshine as it popped out from between the clouds.

Later, as I pondered those moments on the sidewalk, I realized that what we look for determines what we find. I knew that! But I forgot that lesson when I became sidetracked looking for a few shiny and unimportant things. But when God calls us, He sees the finish to what He starts. And He always has our best in mind. Let us look up and keep following.

God who guides us, help me to see a shining token of Your love at the outset of each new journey. I pray this in the loving name of Jesus. Amen.

January 16–22. **Drexel Rankin** served as an ordained minister for more than 35 years with full-time pastorates in Indiana, Alabama, and Kentucky.

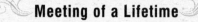

Meeting of a Lifetime

As soon as Joseph appeared before him, he threw his arms around his father and wept for a long time (Genesis 46:29).

Scripture: Genesis 46:28–47:6
Song: "O God, Whose Love Is over All"

Twice in recent months, I have moved. In the early summer, my wife and I downsized when we relocated to our present ranch-style house. Most of our living now is on one floor.

Today, I am only a week away from leaving my present post to begin an early retirement after nearly 40 years of ordained ministry.

Three months ago, we cleaned out our other house. Today I begin the process of cleaning out my church office. I sift through stacks of papers, peruse files in my desk, and clear shelves of both books and publications that I thought I might use someday.

In the process of both moves, I have learned and relearned several truths. A lot of what I save, thinking it is important, really isn't. I've discovered some things I forgot I had. Organization does away with confusion and chaos. New life comes when one cleans up, clears out, and coordinates.

So it is with life. Every once in a while, we need to sort out what is important and what is not important. We must get in touch with "stuff"—or people—we've lost. It can be so poignant, as it was on that amazing day when Joseph threw his arms around long-lost brothers. They had moved far, far apart; now they were face to face, a meeting of a lifetime.

Lord, help me to recognize and to cherish what is important in life, especially those people who come back into my life from long years past. In Jesus' name, amen.

The Blessings of Children

Joseph brought his sons close to [Israel], and his father kissed them and embraced them (Genesis 48:10).

Scripture: Genesis 48:8-16
Song: "There Shall Be Showers of Blessings"

My wife and I spent most of last weekend with our son and his family in Indianapolis. When we are with them, we try to spend as much time with the grandchildren as possible. They grow up so quickly.

While playing with 4-year-old grandson Benjamin on the family room floor, I realized that there are moments in life that I simply do not want to forget. This was one of them.

Benjamin likes trucks. That is certainly an understatement. He has a rather large collection of them. What fascinated me about our playtime that morning was his contentment with having me "play trucks" with him for well over an hour.

All I needed to do was to keep the trucks moving or else he he'd say, "Play trucks with me, Papaw." Move the trucks back and forth on the rug; run the trucks around a track; take the trucks on an imaginary journey under the table. It doesn't matter. Just don't *park* the trucks!

He is so happy, easily entertained, content with simple pastimes. Oh, that I should be as happy and content as a child! I think Benjamin teaches me about important things as I share life with him.

Loving God, help me to see the world and my life through the eyes of a 4-year-old for a while today. Teach me to see the beauty of simple things and the joy of embracing my family. In the name of Jesus, amen.

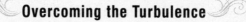

Overcoming the Turbulence

With bitterness archers attacked him; they shot at him with hostility. But his bow remained steady (Genesis 49:23, 24).

Scripture: Genesis 49:22-26
Song: "It Is Well with My Soul"

The glider pilot told about his love for gliding. He explained technique, displayed models of gliders, and showed a video of a flight over the surrounding area. He spoke of the thrill of flying and the silence he experienced when sailing along thousands of feet above ground.

He answered questions about operating a plane that is powered only by air currents. The pilot must understand how the currents move in order to direct the plane to lower or higher altitudes. When asked what he did when he encountered turbulence, he said, "I adjust the glider's altitude." The pilot might choose to drop to a lower altitude to find smoother air, or he might find a thermal—a current of warmer air—and let the thermal raise the plane higher. His preference was to go higher whenever possible. This allowed both an escape from turbulence and the possibility of a longer flight.

Like glider pilots, we choose certain actions or go in certain directions when we encounter turbulence in life. It's an old lesson—one that we have heard countless times before. I need to get some *altitude* and get in touch with the one who offers hope amidst all difficulties.

Father, help me to find the higher plane when I encounter turbulence in my life. In finding strength and guidance from Your hand, may I not be overcome by those difficulties that I encounter in each day. In the name of Your son I pray. Amen.

Capturing Joy

I am about to be gathered to my people (Genesis 49:29).

Scripture: Genesis 49:29–50:6
Song: "For the Beauty of the Earth"

I'm grateful that I was able to spend time with two special people. Lloyd was senior minister where I served as student associate nearly 40 years ago. He was my ministerial mentor. This was a time in my life when I received little support from my parents as I prepared for ministry. So Lloyd and his wife became a surrogate mom and dad as well.

Although we talk on the phone frequently, I had not visited him in Texas for three years. During our last phone conversation, Lloyd asked, "When are you coming to see us?" It was not an idle question.

So my wife and I flew to Dallas and had a wonderful visit with these special people who mean much to me. Lloyd is now 92 and knows that his remaining time is limited. Shortly before we arrived, his doctor told Lloyd that he could no longer drive his car. His wife is in the early stages of Alzheimer's disease.

Lloyd continues to write poetry for almost any occasion. His wife functions as best she can. Both are doing their best to live life to its fullest.

And they are about to be "gathered" to God and His people in a brand new existence. They have been blessed—and have blessed many others. Thanks be to God.

God of joy, help me to cherish those people who mean so much to me. May I not lose sight of the importance of these Christian relationships that help form my life and strengthen me in my journey. In Christ I ask this. Amen.

Through Difficult Times

All Pharaoh's officials accompanied him—the dignitaries of his court and all the dignitaries of Egypt—besides all the members of Joseph's household and his brothers and those belonging to his father's household (Genesis 50:7, 8).

Scripture: Genesis 50:7-14
Song: "Day After Day I Sought the Lord"

The surgeon spoke calmly, but I found his diagnosis unnerving. "I've found two large masses, and I think that one of them—possibly both—are cancerous." He had examined me thoroughly and explained the procedure that would follow.

Within a few days, I underwent cancer surgery. Friends sat in the waiting room with my anxious, frightened wife, as the surgeon completed his skillful work. When I awoke in the recovery room, I saw my wife sitting by my side. And during the days that followed, friends surrounded us both, physically and emotionally.

Many visitors came to my hospital room. Church members assured us of their prayers. From out of state, a prayer shawl arrived from friends in a church that I had served three years earlier. Everywhere we turned, our friends walked with us through this difficult time.

Throughout my years of ministry, I always marveled at the strength people gathered because their friends upheld them in times of death and crisis. Now that I have experienced such support, I understand.

God of hope, even in the darkest of times, You are with me, offering hope and strength. And for the presence of friends in Christ, I give thanks. In His name, amen.

Forgiving

What if Joseph holds a grudge against us and pays us back for all the wrongs we did to him? (Genesis 50:15).

Scripture: Genesis 50:15-26
Song: "Father, Forgive, the Savior Said"

Have you ever received forgiveness before asking for it? I received such a gift.

She and I often disagreed when I was her minister. Laura saw things one way; I saw them another. It all came to a head when she chaired a major project at the church. She felt strongly that things needed to take one direction; I believed they should proceed in another direction. The result was that she and her husband moved their memberships.

Shortly after that decision, I was called to another ministry. Several years passed before I saw her again.

We both were attending the same conference in another city. I rounded the corner of a display area, and there she was, talking to my wife. My first inclination was to duck back around the corner. I chose, rather, to proceed down the aisle and join them.

Her first words to me were: "Can I hug you?"

In that action, I received forgiveness and grace from someone with whom I had unfinished business.

Do we really believe that holding a grudge and not forgiving is unimportant to God? Sadly, we are the ones who suffer the most when we choose not to forgive.

Forgiving God, continue to remind me that Your son's command to forgive is in place for our own good and for the well-being of others. Help me to receive the reward of forgiveness along with its freedom. In the name of Jesus I pray. Amen.

Storms Brewing

Your path led through the sea, your way through the mighty waters, though your footprints were not seen (Psalm 77:19).

Scripture: Psalm 77:11-20
Song: "We Have an Anchor"

"There's a storm brewing around the world," Don announced before we sang "Will Your Anchor Hold in the Storms of Life?" On that Wednesday night at church, Don, as usual, led us in three songs while his wife, Mary, played the organ. Don's statement at first led my thoughts to world conflict, but then the song brought me back to the personal storms of life—particularly the storms in Don's life.

A year ago Don received a kidney transplant, and for the past several months he'd experienced setbacks in recovering. Yet with confidence in his God, Don sang, "We have an anchor that keeps the soul steadfast and sure . . . fastened to the Rock which cannot move."

In Psalm 77 the author asked some tough questions about God's love. Then he remembered the Lord's deeds, particularly the Israelites' flight out of Egypt. The mighty waters of the Red Sea were no problem with God. He led them through on dry land. His "mighty right arm" saved His people. And God continues to bring deliverance through life's storms.

Mighty God, I have no other anchor than You. Help me to testify to others of Your protection and power. In Christ's name I pray. Amen.

January 23–29. **Ann Coker** is happily employed in ministry serving women faced with crisis pregnancies. At home in Terre Haute, Indiana, all conversations are interrupted to watch wildlife.

God Prepares the Way

Joseph was already in Egypt (Exodus 1:5).

Scripture: Exodus 1:1-7
Song: "He Leadeth Me"

The drive out of Wilmore, Kentucky, was less emotional than I'd expected. My husband and I were leaving 17 years of work and friendships in this academic town to return to church ministry in a new place. Soon after arriving in Terre Haute, Indiana, church members and staff greeted us at our new home. The next day we received letters from friends and phone calls from family.

All these "welcome mats" were tangible examples of God's provision set in place beforehand. They were reminders of Scriptures such as: "The Lord your God, who is going before you, will fight for you" (Deuteronomy 1:30); "Before they call I will answer" (Isaiah 65:24); and "The one who calls you is faithful and he will do it" (1 Thessalonians 5:24).

God placed Joseph in Egypt at a strategic time in that part of the world. God made it possible for Joseph, as second in command to Pharaoh, to store up provisions before famine struck the lands. Joseph waited there, ready to answer the physical needs of his father and brothers and eager to restore the family's spiritual bonds through forgiveness. The brothers' actions were meant for evil, but "God intended it for good" (Genesis 50:20).

Father God, Your deeds are always meant for my good, and I know that You watch over my every moment. You go before me and prepare the way for blessings. Help me to trust You as my great provider. In Jesus' name, amen.

The Hand of God I See

In all their hard labor the Egyptians used them ruthlessly (Exodus 1:14).

Scripture: Exodus 1:8-14
Song: "God Moves in a Mysterious Way"

Blessings often come out of hardship. William Cowper was frequently plagued by seasons of depression. But we owe him a debt of gratitude for more than 68 hymns published, along with John Newton's, in the Olney Hymns (1779). Another inspiring story comes to us from the town of Olney, Buckinghamshire, England. The illiterate poor people created beautiful bobbin lace in their cold, dimly lit homes. This artistic work provided a worthy trade for their sustenance and well-being in times of hardship.

Our text tells us how the Egyptians "ruthlessly" forced the Hebrew people into hard labor as slaves. Yet the people continued to multiply and grew stronger in body and spirit. By God's grace, they finally escaped their cruel taskmasters.

After reading through a year's journal entries, I came to the conclusion that sorrows and hard times, as well as joys and blessings, contributed to a unity of mind and spirit. I've noticed a consistent growth pattern, through God's grace, for my husband and me.

I invite you to take some time to rehearse a particular year in your life. See what God has done for and through you. After seeing God's providence you will be able to sing, "The hand of God in all my life I see" (Herbert Buffum).

Lord, I rejoice in those times of privilege You have provided, but I am also thankful that I can see Your hand in the hard times as well. Thank You. In Jesus' name, amen.

Courage to Stand Up

The midwives, however, feared God . . . they let the boys live (Exodus 1:17).

Scripture: Exodus 1:15-22
Song: "I Know Whom I Have Believed"

When talking to youth, I cite two examples of the courage it takes to stand up for what we believe. In February 2002, Judge Charles Pickering was nominated for the 5th Circuit Court of Appeals. Throughout all the grueling proceedings, Judge Pickering did not step aside but simply said, "I'm here."

My second example quotes members of the Christian band, dc Talk. In song they ask, "What will people think?" and singer Michael Tait explains, "That [question] crystallizes our fear of being different." Then he adds, "I know the answer, I don't really care. My life is God's. I've crossed the line from innocent bystander to hard-core participant in what Jesus has called me to. I hope, whatever I do, it makes them think of Jesus."

The Israelite midwives in today's passage had the courage to go against the edict of the king of Egypt because they feared God more. They took a stand and allowed the baby boys to live.

We all have faced tough challenges. What challenges will come to us in the year ahead? We don't know. But we do know that we'll need courage to take a stand and fear God. We can prepare now to build the spiritual reserves necessary for that time of relying on God's truth.

God of truth and light, equip me now to stand up for You and Your way. Fearing You means obedience in times of challenging situations. I trust You to give me the needed courage to be Your witness to the truth. In Christ's name I pray. Amen.

God's Power Displayed

Your right hand, O Lord, was majestic in power. Your right hand, O Lord, shattered the enemy (Exodus 15:6).

Scripture: Exodus 15:4-10
Song: "He Rolled the Sea Away"

Not only did the Israelites cross the Red Sea on dry land, but their enemy in hot pursuit was drowned in the same sea. The *Good News Bible* translates the event: "He threw Egypt's army and its chariots into the sea." The *New International Version*® states that "he has hurled [them] into the sea" (v. 4). God performed a double miracle for His people and their enemy.

God's mighty right hand rolled the sea back and then rolled it back again onto the enemy. That same power is available for each of us today. God can and does roll back the troubles that would drown us, and He also sinks our fears and doubts like lead in the waves.

After children's choir practice at our former church, the leader would allow the children to choose a song. Invariably someone would shout out, "Pharaoh, Pharaoh." I'm not sure what they liked more—the catchy words, the fast tempo, or the motions—but the children would sing enthusiastically. These same children, now in high school and college, have the opportunity to take the message of those catchy words and form their resolve to serve the Lord no matter what. The miracle of God's deliverance is a message for young and old.

Mighty God, I read about Your displays of power in Bible times. In my own life You have delivered me from evil. I am also aware that You work within me to strengthen my resolve to serve You and others. For all this I am grateful. In Jesus' name, amen.

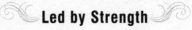

Led by Strength

In your unfailing love you will lead the people you have redeemed. In your strength you will guide them to your holy dwelling (Exodus 15:13).

Scripture: Exodus 15:11-18
Song: "A Mighty Fortress Is Our God"

In the movie version of J.R.R. Tolkien's trilogy, *The Lord of the Rings*, the hobbits first meet Strider not far from their shire. This robed suspicious character would become their leader and trusted friend. Along the journey they learn that he is Aragorn, the one who would eventually lead the allied troops of Arnor and Gondor against the dark lord.

In one stirring scene, Aragorn faces his army with sword lifted high. He speaks courage and then turns to lead them into a fierce battle. Led by his strength, they are triumphant together. Later, Aragorn is crowned High King of the Reunited Kingdom.

God leads His redeemed people each day into the battles of life. Guided by His love and power, we go forth to conquer the enemy within and without. In His strength we can be victorious against sin and selfishness. We learn from childhood that "we are weak and He is strong," for we are confident not in ourselves but in Christ alone. He has the power to break any stronghold that would thwart victory.

When we put on the full armor of God we are led through the battles of this life into an eternal home, His "holy dwelling."

Eternal God, I cannot go through one day without Your presence, power, and provision. I trust in Your strength to guide me victoriously through each day and on into eternity. Thanks. In Christ's name I pray. Amen.

The Theme of My Song

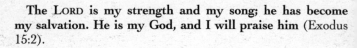

The LORD is my strength and my song; he has become my salvation. He is my God, and I will praise him (Exodus 15:2).

Scripture: Exodus 15:1-5, 19-26
Song: "All Hail the Power of Jesus' Name"

I remember the day well. I was reading my Bible that morning, a routine practice, when the words began to sing off the page. A newness of life enveloped me as I read, "Sing to the Lord a new song" (Isaiah 42:10). A simple verse, yet it became mine. I backed up and sang aloud the verses. My servant king had put a song in my heart, not for the first time, but fresh for that day.

In today's passage we find a woman whose heart was so full of joy that she had to burst out in praise for her God. Miriam, Aaron's sister, led in song, and all the women joined her. The background for her song was the mighty deliverance of the Israelites from their longtime oppressive enemy. God's miracle allowed them to walk across the dried-up bed of the Red Sea. When the Egyptian army tried to follow, the men, chariots, and horses were drowned as God rolled the sea back over them. What a cause for rejoicing!

In our day we have not experienced such a miracle, but we have many reasons for rejoicing. That day I found the verse about a new song was an unexpected blessing. Let's thank God now for those times when we have found a new song.

Mighty Deliverer, I thank You for all those times You have given me unexpected moments of rejoicing. You have shown me how You rescued me from so many temptations. Give me the grace to sing to You a new song today. In Jesus' name, amen.

 "Only the Living God"

They have no knowledge that set up the wood of their graven image, and pray unto a god that cannot save (Isaiah 45:20, *King James Version*).

Scripture: Isaiah 45:20-25
Song: "He Is Lord"

Idols are made of wood and other materials too, of course. I once made a piece of plastic my idol, which my dear mother had often warned me about. In ignorance, I thought this idol could save me, as well as certain family members. However, even after using my credit card to the max, I still came up empty. Instead of the happiness and fulfillment I had hoped for, it brought misery, pain, and several trips to court for nonpayment.

Standing before the judge, I remembered my mother's words. "You're not giving God your full attention, because you're too busy thinking about your bills. Don't you know God wants you to always put Him first?"

I certainly know that now. Even more so, I've committed to memory Matthew 6:33: "Seek first his kingdom and his righteousness, and all these things will be given to you as well."

I realized that day in court that "these things" include God's grace and mercy, which I desperately needed. Quietly and earnestly, I communicated with the living God, and He saved me.

Heavenly Father, how faithful You are! Thank You for hearing my prayer and offering Your liberating truth. Help me to keep You first in my life. Let me always remember Your grace and mercy and hold fast to it. In the precious name of Jesus, amen.

January 30, 31. **Jimmie Oliver Fleming,** of Chester, Virginia, recently obtained a copy of her song, "Winter in June," that she wrote 42 years ago.

God Is Not Surprised

Righteousness from God comes through faith in Jesus Christ to all who believe. There is no difference, for all have sinned and fall short of the glory of God (Romans 3:22, 23).

Scripture: Romans 3:21-26
Song: "Whiter than Snow"

As I write this devotional, a big chill is sweeping across the United States and other parts of the world. People admit being surprised by the frigid winter weather. The weather reporters may be more surprised than anyone else. While they don't say for sure that weather like this has never occurred in certain places, they seem to agree, "We're reporting some of the coldest temperatures on record."

God keeps records as well, and He isn't surprised by anything that happens in the entire universe. God knew about all the events that would occur when He created all things.

Likewise, God knew that Adam and Eve would sin in the Garden of Eden. Today's Scripture reminds us that all have sinned. None of us is exempt. Yet God wants us to confess our sins and receive His forgiveness and cleansing (see 1 John 1:9).

In Isaiah 1:18, we find these words, "Come now, let us reason together," says the Lord. "Though your sins are like scarlet, they shall be as white as snow."

The choice is ours. We have a second chance.

Almighty and gracious Father, thank You for opening my eyes to my sin nature and giving me a second chance for eternal life. Help me to keep my eyes opened and not let my lies of denial or stubbornness hinder me from confessing my disobedience and shortcomings to You. In Jesus' name, amen.

DEVOTIONS®

FEBRUARY

His divine power has given us everything we need for life and godliness through our knowledge of him.

—*2 Peter 1:3*

Gary Allen, Editor   **Margaret Williams,** Project Editor   Photo © Liquid Library

DEVOTIONS® is published quarterly by Standard Publishing, Cincinnati, Ohio, www.standardpub.com. © 2010 by Standard Publishing. All rights reserved. Topics based on the Home Daily Bible Readings, International Sunday School Lessons. © 2008 by the Committee on the Uniform Series. Printed in the U.S.A. All Scripture quotations, unless otherwise indicated, are taken from the *HOLY BIBLE, NEW INTERNATIONAL VERSION®. NIV®.* Copyright © 1973, 1978, 1984 by Biblica Inc.™ Used by permission of Zondervan. All rights reserved. Where noted, Scripture quotations are from the following, used with the permission of the copyright holders, all rights reserved. *Contemporary English Version (CEV),* © 1991, 1992, 1995 American Bible Society. *Holy Bible, New Living Translation (NLT),* © 1996. Tyndale House Publishers. *King James Version, (KJV),* public domain.

Justified Before God

Everyone who exalts himself will be humbled, and he who humbles himself will be exalted (Luke 18:14).

Scripture: Luke 18:9-14
Song: "He Lifted Me"

"It says it right here, Honey," the husband said to his wife. "So you have to believe it." However, the wife's waning faith would not permit her to believe the information just yet. Where would she get the additional money for the printer cartridge she needed to finish her latest writing assignment? "I should have tried harder to make the store manager see my point of view," she told her husband. "I gave up too soon."

"No, you did exactly right," he said. "Besides, it's not about your point of view, but about God's. Your attitude when you spoke to the store manager set a good example, believe me."

"I do believe you," his wife replied as she read the verse for herself. "I tell you, this sinner, not the Pharisee, returned home justified before God" (Luke 18:14, *New Living Translation*).

She suddenly felt justified. What's more, she checked the old cartridge in her printer again—and discovered plenty of ink to finish her assignment. Even though the office supply store manager hadn't honored her request for a discount on the brand name cartridge, after being out of stock with the store brand, God had still made a way.

Father God, help me to believe and trust Your Word and know that I can personally apply it to my life's situations. In Jesus' name, I humbly pray. Amen.

February 1–5. **Jimmie Oliver Fleming,** of Chester, Virginia, recently obtained a copy of her song, "Winter in June," that she wrote 42 years ago.

Peer Pressure

I am astonished that you are so quickly deserting the one who called you by the grace of Christ and are turning to a different gospel (Galatians 1:6).

Scripture: Galatians 1:1-10
Song: "I Cannot Tell"

The 8-year-old boy had heard a big word from his teacher, yet he fully understood it: *astonished*. He had often heard this very word from his father, who kept him while his mother worked the night shift. He had also heard his mother say that his father should become a teacher. However, Dad remained in sales and held five different jobs, while Mom held the same job for 10 years.

Calculating this, the boy realized that in two years, he would also be 10. Now he was still 8 and had been given the responsibility of supervising his elementary school classroom for a moment while his teacher stepped out to the office. On returning, she did not hold back her surprise. All of the children were running around in the classroom, in complete chaos. "I am astonished!" she declared.

"Me too," the 8-year-old quietly responded. "But I got carried away with my peers."

Perhaps the Galatians did this as well—they so willingly believed something other than Paul's gospel message of pure grace.

O God, the king of glory, thank You for my free will, but please let it connect with Your will. Keep me seeking to know more about You. Let my light shine before others so that they may see Your good works and be encouraged to serve You wholeheartedly. In Christ's name I pray. Amen.

Land of Make Believe?

I certify you, brethren, that the gospel which was preached of me is not after man (Galatians 1:11, *King James Version*).

Scripture: Galatians 1:11-24
Song: "Jesus Is Real"

Have you ever been accused of making things up, of "living in a fantasy world"? Sure, it's easy for others to challenge our faith. And they may find it hard to listen when we readily give reasons for our beliefs. But we must not give up.

Paul says that he received the gospel by revelation from Jesus Christ. If we receive the gospel in this manner, it also must come by faith. Hebrews 11:1 says, "Now faith is the substance of things hoped for, the evidence of things not seen" (*KJV*).

We can exercise our faith by reading the Word of God and receiving the truth of it. Jesus still speaks through His Word. And, no, it is not something simply made up.

A 6-year-old girl mentioned to her father that Grandfather had read a library book to her that she had brought along on her visit. After telling her father some of the things in the book, the father eagerly asked, "And then what happened?"

The girl smiled and replied, "Read it to me and find out."

Great answer. And it can also apply to knowing the truth of the gospel. Let us read it, know it, and receive it by faith.

Dear Savior and Lord, how I like following Your Word. How tasty and revealing it is when I open myself to receive it. May I feast on this delicious marrow at every opportunity. Above all, keep me reminded of the rich nourishment of Your Word for my soul. In the name of Christ I pray. Amen.

The Right Hand

For God, who was at work in the ministry of Peter as an apostle to the Jews, was also at work in my ministry as apostle to the Gentiles (Galatians 2:8)

Scripture: Galatians 2:6-10
Song: "Help Somebody Today"

As I started to write this devotional, I thought of my old friend Betty from Long Island, New York. She once shared with me that she had a problem with some members at her church—something similar to what Paul was facing with the Galatians. Still, Betty hung in there and got the job done in spite of their legalistic opposition. She simply did what she believed God wanted, much as the apostle Paul did when he brought the gospel to the Gentiles.

Receiving help and acceptance from the other apostles also made a big difference. However, first these apostles had to believe that Paul was actually preaching the true gospel of grace and that his message was genuine. They then gave Paul and Barnabas the "right hand of fellowship" (v. 9).

I'm sure all of us at times have needed a helping hand, and in the same way, have given a helping hand. The "right hand" in comparison to the "wrong hand" is always better. Indeed, as our song for today proclaims: "Look all around you, find someone in need, Help somebody today!"

Almighty and gracious Father, thank You for this day and for this moment in time. I am so grateful that You have allowed me to see it. Help me use it to the fullest. Help me give whomever I can a helping hand, knowing that I have given the right hand. I pray this prayer in the name of Jesus, my Savior and Lord. Amen.

A Faith Test

I have been crucified with Christ and I no longer live, but Christ lives in me. The life I live in the body, I live by faith in the Son of God, who loved me and gave himself for me (Galatians 2:20).

Scripture: Galatians 2:15-21
Song: "I Am Crucified with Christ"

"Paul, are you sure about this? Do you really know what you're talking about?" These two questions could be asked of the apostle Paul today, just as some may have asked them in his day.

We may wrestle with certain things that we already know the Lord wants us to do. Yet what happens when we don't obey and follow through on our guidance from Him? As one lady put it, "We're subject to losing blessing."

I think this may have happened to me on more than one occasion. I'm trying hard to wake up and be wiser. I'm sure that God will grant me a more willing heart, if I ask. I also know it requires asking in faith. Admittedly it is tough to live by faith at times, but God's Word says we must. The apostle Paul says it too, of course, and is therefore setting an example.

As we reflect on Paul's words in today's verse, we can also reflect on and apply his words from Philippians 4:13, "I can do everything through him who gives me strength."

Jesus, how sweet and precious is Your name. I am thankful that I can call on Your name. Even when I don't say it aloud, I know You still hear me, and I know that You are my friend always. Thank You. In the name of Jesus I pray. Amen.

Not Alone

I have chosen him, so that he will direct his children and his household after him to keep the way of the LORD by doing what is right and just, so that the LORD will bring about for Abraham what he has promised him (Genesis 18:19).

Scripture: Genesis 18:16-21
Song: "I Was There to Hear Your Borning Cry"

How many times had I read the 19th verse found in Genesis 18? But it wasn't until I was holding my newborn son in my arms that I was overwhelmed by the meaning of those words. It wasn't just Abraham who was to teach his family to obey God. Now I too was charged with the task of teaching my son about "the way of the Lord." Who would help me teach him "what is right and just"? Was I really up to this task?

My parents and my in-laws came to meet their new grandson. Each held him close, whispering a sweet welcome in his ear. Friends visited to celebrate his birth too. Later I reflected on the many ways my family, friends, and colleagues had touched my life. When there was difficulty or pain or uncertainty, they prayed for me—interceding with God on my behalf, on my son's behalf. It was then that I knew I was not alone—that he was not alone. I knew God was with us . . . even as He had been with Abraham and his children.

Lord God, I ask You to guide me in a life of faithfulness to Your teachings. Help me to do what is right and just. Give me a listening ear and a tender heart to hear the cries of those in need. In Christ's name I pray. Amen.

February 6–12. **Viola Ruelke Gommer** is a nurse, freelance writer, and photographer who lives and works in Dallas, Pennsylvania.

It's a Rule!

I am the Lord your God, and you must obey my teachings. Obey them and you will live. I am the Lord (Leviticus 18:4, 5, *Contemporary English Version*).

Scripture: Leviticus 18:1-5
Song: "Dear Lord, Lead Me Day by Day"

My 3-year-old granddaughter came rushing into the living room. She climbed up into the oversized chair, crossing her arms in defiance. Her usually bright eyes were almost on fire with anger. "Maddie, what's the problem?" I asked. "Don't you want to play outside with the others?"

She didn't even look up at me. "I was playing with them. They made me mad."

"But why are you sitting in here?"

"Mommy says that when I get mad I have to take a time out. It's to get control. It's a rule."

A few minutes passed. "Are you still angry? Are you in control now? If you are, you may go play with your friends."

Maddie looked up at me with her big brown eyes; they were bright again. She smiled as she slid off the chair. Running to the screen door, she called, "I'm coming."

Maddie gave me quite a lesson that morning. She obeyed her mother's teachings, even when her mother wasn't present. How often do I just do my thing? live it my way? I know the Lord wants me to remember His teachings. He wants me to obey His Word. When I do, no matter the circumstances, I am fully alive.

Lord, You are my God. Guide me through my day. Help me to obey Your teachings. Help me to do Your will and live in Your presence. In Christ's name I pray. Amen.

A Command Requires a Reply

Cursed is anyone who does not affirm the terms of this law by obeying them. And all the people will reply, "Amen" (Deuteronomy 27:26, *New Living Translation*).

Scripture: Deuteronomy 27:15-26
Song: "Leader of Faithful Souls"

The very first morning of the new semester I walked around the classroom handing each student the course guidelines. Together we reviewed the course credits, description, dated readings and the assignments. The requirements for each assignment were explained in detail.

Then I asked the students three questions. First, "Is this the class you registered to take?" Second, "Do you understand the requirements and expectations?" And third, "Do you agree to meet the demands written in the guidelines?" Finally, I asked the students to raise their hands to affirm their personal understanding and commitment—and all the students replied, "Yes!"

That morning's review of the guidelines provided the students stepping-stones to success on their educational path. These stones would be a guide to a positive learning experience.

As I read the Scripture for today, I realized it offered the Israelite people just such stepping-stones to maneuver through the difficulties and dangers of their life journey. Once the commands were heard, and their meaning understood, the people replied, "Amen. Yes! Yes! Yes!" To follow the commands would bring the people grace and blessings.

Lord God, I hear Your voice. I answer, "Yes, absolutely." I trust You to guide my steps on this journey. Through Christ I pray. Amen.

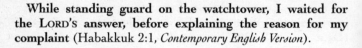

Watching and Waiting

While standing guard on the watchtower, I waited for the LORD'S answer, before explaining the reason for my complaint (Habakkuk 2:1, *Contemporary English Version*).

Scripture: Habakkuk 2:1-5
Song: "Jesus, Use Me"

My friend shared her decision to take a year's sabbatical. Marcy believed she needed to withdraw from her current staff role in an important ministry. She wanted time apart to discover what plans God had in store for her.

How could she possibly just walk away? She would be without a salary, a home, and health insurance. Where would the money come from to pay her bills? Marcy said, "I have some savings that I'll use very carefully. All I have to do is find a place to live—and wait for God's answer."

Marcy contacted a director of a retreat center. He was willing to give her room and board in exchange for volunteer work. Marcy's time at the retreat center became a watchtower experience for her—waiting in faith, trusting the Lord to answer, in His time. It was a time of discernment, questioning, and resting in the Spirit's promptings.

Near the year's end, she received a phone call. "I think you might be the person we are looking for to plant a new ministry. Would you consider the challenge? Think about it. Pray about it. Then call me."

Lord, help me find time for reflection. Time to learn how I am to serve You. I look to You to strengthen my faith. I look to You to give my life direction. In the name of Christ I pray. Amen.

Not Defeated

Call to remembrance the former days, in which, after ye were illuminated, ye endured a great fight of afflictions (Hebrews 10:32, 33, *King James Version*).

Scripture: Hebrews 10:32-39
Song: "Be Still, My Soul"

How do you hold back six feet of water? You don't! The river's water rushed through our home as we hurriedly left. When the waters receded, we tried to get back into the house. The swollen doors wouldn't let us in, so we struggled to enter through a window.

The toppled furniture was covered with river mud. The air smelled sour, rancid from rotting food. And pairs of the children's shoes floated in the muddy water. At the sight of them I whisper, "Lord, thank You for the children's escape. But what do we do now?"

Strangers came from afar to help us with the cleanup. They brought cleaning supplies, along with food and water to sustain themselves—and us. Their hands were always ready to help lift our household furnishings onto the pile of rubble at the curb. They shared our suffering and pain. Their presence gave us strength and courage to tackle the day's tasks. Those strangers became friends who are remembered and cherished to this day.

We were not destroyed. The water took only our belongings.

O Lord, may I offer aid to others as it has been offered to me. May I share my faith as it has been shared with me. May I walk close to those in need as others have walked with me. Only with their help and Yours did I survive. I pray this prayer in the precious name of Jesus my Lord. Amen.

What Must I Do?

"If you want to be perfect, go, sell your possessions and give to the poor, and you will have treasure in heaven. Then come, follow me." When the young man heard this, he went away sad, because he had great wealth (Matthew 19:21, 22).

Scripture: Matthew 19:16-26
Song: "Savior, 'Tis a Full Surrender"

Win was a young man, just beginning to climb the corporate ladder. The company president soon noticed his work, and his salary was bumped up to a level he'd only dreamed about.

Win was also active in his church, involved with its children and youth. One evening, the minister asked, "Win, have you thought of going into the ministry? You share your faith with the youth so easily." Win was speechless. He was just touching the edge of success in his corporate life, and this was not the time to change careers. What could this man be thinking? The minister said, "Will you pray about it?"

Win struggled with the minister's question. He thought about his work, and all the possibilities it offered. The words of the rich young man haunted him—"What must I do?"

But, Lord, this isn't the right time, Win thought. *My life is just taking off. I'm not the right person. I don't have the talents needed. This wasn't in my plans.*

Finally, God only knows why, Win prayed, "Lord, I surrender my life and all my possessions. I want to follow You." For the next 50 years, he served the Lord he decided to follow.

God, I do not want to walk away sorrowfully from You. Help me release all that I hold tight—my money, comfort, possessions, and complacency. In Jesus' name, amen.

Living by Faith

The righteous will live by faith (Galatians 3:11).

Scripture: Galatians 3:1-14
Song: "'Tis So Sweet to Trust in Jesus"

Mother sat at the dining room table ready to fill her budget envelopes. She picked up dad's pay envelope and counted the cash with great care. The amount was not always the same. It depended on the dollars that came into the mission's ministry. No matter the amount, the first envelope to be filled was labeled Tithe. Those that followed were labeled Food, Electricity, Insurance, Gas, and Bus Fare. It wasn't easy for her to make the meager amount carry the household to the month's end.

I noticed she was writing, crossing some things out, then rewriting. "Mom, what's wrong? You keep redoing whatever it is your writing." Mother didn't look up as she answered, "I'm not sure how we will manage this month. Once more there isn't enough to pay our bills."

"Can't we borrow out of the tithe?" I asked.

She spun around in her chair, "That isn't our money. The Lord has always provided for us. He will again." End of conversation.

Mother had been in this tight spot before. And as in the past, she took God at His Word and simply lived by faith. He always provided enough in His time. He would again—and He did.

Eternal God, forgive my wobbly faith and my shallow trust in You. Make me strong to walk life's path by faith. Fill me with trust. You know my needs before I even ask. Enlarge my heart with gratitude. What You have given is always enough. In the name of Your Son, my Savior, I pray. Amen.

Soaking Up the Son

I will make you fruitful; I will make nations of you, and kings will come from you (Genesis 17:6).

Scripture: Genesis 17:1-8
Song: "Make Me a Blessing"

Vineyards abound in the tiny village of Berneck, Switzerland, the sides of the mountains dotted with homes and vines that are both hundreds of years old. Some vines sprawl up the sides of houses, their roots extremely thick from years of steady growth and pruning.

Why is pruning necessary? If the plant is allowed to grow out of control, its leaves begin to shade the vine. Without direct sunlight, the fruit will not ripen properly. And in the shaded environment, disease and insects will invade.

Jeremiah 17:8 promises that when we trust in the Lord, we will never fail to bear fruit. We can do nothing, on our own, to cause fruit to grow. Only God can do that. Though shade may be more comfortable at times, our responsibility is to prune the vine—to cut out those things in our lives that might cause us to veer from the light of God's will for us.

When pruned and freed from hindrances, branches faithfully bear fruit every year. They are connected to the vine and allow the life of the vine to flow through them.

Thank You, **Heavenly Father,** for the beauty of Your creation—the sweetness of fruit that only You can produce. Thank You for Your promise to produce fruit in my life. In the holy name of Jesus, my Lord and Savior, I pray. Amen.

February 13–19. **Barb Haley** has worked as an elementary school teacher and private piano instructor. She and her husband have three grown children and live near San Antonio, Texas.

Is It Working for You?

God has raised this Jesus to life, and we are all witnesses of the fact (Acts 2:32).

Scripture: Acts 2:32-39
Song: "He Took My Sins Away"

Witnesses come to the courtroom to testify about things they have seen and heard. No one is interested in what witnesses *think* happened. Rather, we want to hear what a witness has experienced firsthand.

We are called to be witnesses of the gospel of Christ — to share God's message of grace and salvation with others. But many folks aren't interested. How can we invite them to listen?

The other day I was studying a fiction-writing book on creating settings that readers won't skip over. The secret comes in combining facts with emotions. Describe the most fascinating, romantic, or terrifying location in the world. No one really cares until you somehow connect the setting to a character's feelings — how the location affects the character personally.

When I read this, I immediately thought about how this relates to my Christian witness. While others may disregard or debate the things I share about God, no one can argue with my experience of Him. When I get real about how Christ has touched my life personally, others begin to listen. They want to hear that what I have experienced firsthand is working for me.

Lord God of all, You do so much for me. You saved me from my sins, filled me with Your Holy Spirit, and provide daily guidance, peace, and joy. Place others in my path that I might introduce them to You. May they too begin to enjoy this abundant life in You. In Jesus' name, amen.

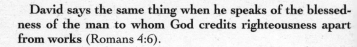

The Heart of the Matter

David says the same thing when he speaks of the blessedness of the man to whom God credits righteousness apart from works (Romans 4:6).

Scripture: Romans 4:1-8
Song: "Think About His Love"

My doctor friend, raised in an extremely legalistic home, turned his back on the Lord. He declared that life was much easier and more enjoyable without all the restrictions of Christianity. I explained the difference between religion and a personal relationship with God. But my friend just laughed and teased me about making him my "project" in order to earn a reward in Heaven.

"Why are you willing to spend such an unbelievable amount of hours at the hospital as a doctor?" I asked him. "Is it only for the paycheck you receive once a month?"

"Of course not," he answered. "Sure, I like the money, but my heart is in my work. I like to help hurting people."

"So, does the fact that you get paid make your dedication any less genuine or heartfelt?"

Checkmate. For a true Christian, our reward is simply that, a reward that is the natural result of our activity in the kingdom. But we are not working our way into Heaven. "For it is by grace you have been saved, through faith . . . it is the gift of God—not by works, so that no one can boast" (Ephesians 2:8, 9).

Dear Lord, Your unconditional love is so rich. Please help me share this love with others. Use my life, my testimony, to lead them to a relationship with You, not a set of rules and rewards. In Christ's name I pray. Amen.

New Clothes for a New Creation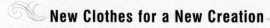

All of you who were baptized into Christ have clothed yourselves with Christ (Galatians 3:27).

Scripture: Galatians 3:19-29
Song: "Purify My Heart"

Easter is exciting for kids—egg hunts, candy baskets, etc. But my favorite childhood memory was my new outfit—frilly dress, socks, and shoes. How special I felt in a totally new outfit.

Looking back, I realize how the new outfit symbolizes the meaning of Easter. Christ lived, died, and rose again that we might become a new creation in Him.

Many people say they believe the gospel, but they don't "walk the talk"—refusing to turn and pursue a new path.

Others desire new life, but aren't willing to give up the old one. Imagine putting fresh clothes on top of soiled ones. The smell remains. The rumpled look will soon show through. And when the layers restrict and grow uncomfortable, the clothes most likely will be discarded and forgotten.

The Bible says we who are baptized into Christ should clothe ourselves with Him. We must consciously remove the clothing of the world—confess our sins, avoid temptation, and examine ourselves to be sure we have surrendered our lives to the Lord. Then, like a child on Easter morning, we can eagerly clothe ourselves in the love and life of Christ.

Lord, thank You for freshness of life in You. Thank You that every day is a new beginning. Old things are passed away; behold, all things are new. Search my heart. Remove that which is not of You. Dress me only in Your love and service. In the precious name of Jesus, amen.

Smarter Than the Average Fish

Those people are zealous to win you over, but for no good. What they want is to alienate you from us, so that you may be zealous for them (Galatians 4:17).

Scripture: Galatians 4:12-20
Song: "Thy Way, Not Mine, O Lord"

Bass are smart fish. But with modern technology, fishermen are smarter. Especially when they use lighted lures that blink blood-red in the water. Fish strike, and the rest is . . . dinner.

When Paul preached the gospel, many living in Galatia followed Christ. It couldn't have been easy to set aside years of teaching about the Law—the truth of the past. No wonder these believers wavered after Paul left.

The religious leaders of the day set the lure, hoping to alienate these new believers from Paul's way of faith. They tried to draw the Galatians back into a life of restriction and bondage to the very law from which Jesus set them free.

As we mature, we often discover that what we believed in the past has changed. When this happens, choosing faith over familiarity takes courage and fortitude.

Consider the influences in your life. Are they leading you where you really want to go? Don't float passively along in life, chasing any lure that looks good. Determine what you stand for and be prepared to step outside your comfort zone to maintain your position.

Dear Lord, life can be tough—especially in a world full of questionable influences. Open my eyes that I might see You better, that I might know the truth and recognize that which is contrary to Your Word. Guard my heart today! In Christ I pray. Amen.

The Yoke's on Us

It is for freedom that Christ has set us free. Stand firm, then, and do not let yourselves be burdened again by a yoke of slavery (Galatians 5:1).

Scripture: Galatians 4:28–5:1
Song: "Standing on the Promises"

In 2 Chronicles 20:17, the Lord reassures the Israelites heading into battle. "Take up your positions; stand firm and see the deliverance the Lord will give you." Now that's my kind of God. Just stand back in the storm and let God speak to the winds.

Reality? Not usually. While God is more than able, He knows we need to battle the winds to grow stronger in Him.

Standing firm is not a passive activity. Some circumstances frighten and discourage us, tempting us to turn and run. Other circumstances confuse us, testing our balance and making it difficult to hold our position. But the Lord says to stand firm. And not only that—He cautions us not to become burdened again by a yoke of slavery.

Picture a team of oxen joined by the wooden beam across their shoulders. It yokes them together, forcing them to carry the same load and travel in the same direction. Christ came to set us free from the that kind of yoke. We don't have to carry a crippling load of guilt and shame. We don't have to be pulled along in darkness and discouragement. Rather, let's slip into the yoke of Christ. He will carry the bulk of the load and lead us in the best direction for our lives.

Dear Lord, thank You for Your love, guidance, and strength. I humbly accept Your yoke—Your plans for my life, day by day. In Jesus' name, amen.

Eagle-Bone Whistle

Because you are sons, God sent the spirit of His Son into our hearts, the Spirit who calls out, "Abba, Father" (Galatians 4:6).

Scripture: Galatians 3:15-18; 4:1-7
Song: "Instruments of Your Peace"

God blesses us with intelligence and the ability to reason. So when should we move ahead in our own understanding, and when should we seek guidance and wisdom from above?

Native Americans speak of the ulna—a hollow bone from the eagle's wing, used to make whistles. This bone, they teach, waits to be formed and filled with breath that will produce music. We are like that bone, waiting to be filled with the breath of the Holy Spirit, ready to sing a song of joy and deliverance to a world of lonely, hurting people.

Sadly, our own knowledge and ideas sometime get in the way. We fill our minds with myriad opinions and beliefs, too busy to line them up with the Word of God. Then our tune gets mixed up with God's.

In 2 Samuel 7, King David was disturbed about living in a palace when the ark of God remained in a tent. The prophet Nathan answered, "Whatever you have in mind, go ahead and do it, for the Lord is with you." But Nathan spoke presumptuously out of his own wisdom. God rebuked him that night and told him that He did not want David to build the temple but his son Solomon. Like Nathan we need to take our own ideas to God for His approval.

Abide in me, **Heavenly Father,** and teach me each day to better recognize and understand Your voice. In the name of Your Son, my Savior, I pray. Amen.

A Generous Pouring

He saved us through the washing of rebirth and renewal by the Holy Spirit, whom he poured out on us generously through Jesus Christ our Savior (Titus 3:5, 6).

Scripture: Titus 3:1-7
Song: "Let the Beauty of Jesus Be Seen in Me"

This year we've had an unusual number of snowstorms. By mid-February, we had more than three times the usual amount. While I have tired of shoveling, I'd have to say it's been a beautiful season, nonetheless.

The drifts and seams of snow across the fields bear the markings of the wind. The overhanging edges curl at the top of the banks, sifting below the breaks of fence and grass. I wonder at the endless patterns, the dips, the smooth openings around the base of posts and trees. Such scenes would be impossible with just a bare dusting of snow.

Such is the working in our hearts of the generous outpouring of the Holy Spirit. Sent to be near to us, to be our guide and comforter, the Holy Spirit did not come to us in tiny, not-quite-enough rations. Instead, we have been so blessed with the very nature and presence of God, so that our former nature might be joyfully overwhelmed.

The Spirit of the Lord indwells us. We cannot but bear in our lives the constant markings of His lovely character.

Help me, **Holy God**, to always embrace the moving, sifting, refining, shaping work of Your presence. In the name of the Father, the Son, and the Holy Spirit, I pray. Amen.

February 20–26. **Doc Arnett** and his wife of 20 years, Randa, live in St. Joseph, Missouri. They both work at Highland (Kansas) Community College.

Shielded by His Power

Through faith [we] are shielded by God's power until the coming of the salvation that is ready to be revealed in the last time (1 Peter 1:5).

Scripture: 1 Peter 1:1-5
Song: "The Battle Belongs to the Lord"

It was a time of incredible turmoil: one of our children had just suffered a minor brush with the law, another was being released from treatment. And my career seemed stagnant, while our budget had taken more hits than a crash-test dummy. My almost lifelong struggle with depression held me teetering at the edge of the chasm. Then, my wife ended up in the hospital.

I couldn't help but think of an old joke. " 'Cheer up,' they told me, 'Things could be worse.' So, I cheered up. And sure enough, things got worse."

Just then, when it seemed that I had every excuse in the world to take a running jump, with a quadruple gainer, into the pit of despair, God gave me a miracle of faith.

Somehow, in the midst of all of this, I felt an inexplicable calmness and confidence. "Everything will be OK." He lifted me above the chaos. I experienced the peace that passes understanding, knowing that a power beyond "mind over matter" had taken hold of me. Without having any idea how all of these things could possibly work out, I still knew, absolutely, that they would. And they did.

Dear Lord and Savior, help me to remember that I have not been abandoned, not been deserted, not been left on my own. Help me always to seek safety behind the shield of faith. In Jesus' name I pray. Amen.

Empowered for Life and Godliness

His divine power has given us everything we need for life and godliness through our knowledge of him who called us by his own glory and goodness (2 Peter 1:3).

Scripture: 2 Peter 1:3-8
Song: "More Love, More Power"

For many years, I did my remodeling and woodworking projects with a small jigsaw that I'd bought back when I was still in school. But when the local hardware store put their industrial model reciprocating saw on sale, I decided to give that a try.

My very next project required cutting a circular hole through a double layer of wood siding. It would have taken me at least 15 minutes with my little jigsaw. But the new tool ripped through the two inches of wood in less than a minute. I could hardly believe it. I imagined all of the extra time and effort I'd spent over the years working with that undersized, underpowered tool.

I also struggled with life, trying to accomplish with human effort what cannot be accomplished with human effort. I tried to live the abundant life and to be godly without the power that God supplies through the Holy Spirit.

Yes, as Peter says, we must "make every effort" (v. 5). But rather than using the feeble tools of self-improvement, we can lay hold of divine power. That enables us to "participate in the divine nature and escape the corruption in the world" (v. 4).

Dear Lord, by Your Word You spoke into existence this very universe. By Your Holy Spirit, You healed sickness, cast out demons, and conquered death. Help me to rely upon Your power for everything I need for life and godliness. Through Christ, amen.

Demonstrate That Faith!

The only thing that counts is faith expressing itself through love (Galatians 5:6).

Scripture: Galatians 5:2-6
Song: "They'll Know We Are Christians by Our Love"

The year was 1982, the occasion was the World's Fair. The place—Knoxville, Tennessee, and western Kentucky. Two teenagers from our small congregation in Calloway County had agreed to go and help work a booth for our denomination. They were there on their own, several hundred miles away. As the weeks passed, at each church service back in Kentucky we would remember them in our prayers, "Lord, bless Wayne and Nick."

One Sunday, our elderly minister caught every one of us completely off guard. "I've noticed how you folks keep praying for these young men, and that's good." Then he paused and added, "But you need to start wrapping those prayers in five-dollar-bills and send them to those boys."

Certainly we ought to always pray, not only for those we love and who love us, but also for those who despise and mistreat us. But we should never allow ourselves to think that believing is a substitute for doing. Yes, Scripture warns those who rely upon the deeds of the flesh as a means of earning salvation. But let us also remember: God calls those who rely upon grace to *demonstrate* their faith through expressions of love.

Dear Lord, help me to demonstrate my faith through my prayers and through my actions. May I imitate Your example of love by yielding myself completely to the working and leading of Your Holy Spirit. In Jesus' name, amen.

Freedom . . . to Serve

You, my brothers, were called to be free. But do not use your freedom to indulge the sinful nature; rather, serve one another in love (Galatians 5:13).

Scripture: Galatians 5:7-15
Song: "O to Be Like Thee"

Most church members would be a bit surprised to know that their minister was enthusiastically watching a PBS documentary, "Moonshiners, Rumrunners, and Bootleggers." Blame it on my culture and those misty hills around Kentucky Lake.

At any rate, a quote from a history professor during the program provoked my interest. In explaining the historic willingness of folks in the more remote parts of Appalachia to ignore some of the finer points of law, he explained, "We are a nation founded on rebellion. Independence and rejection of authority are part of our national character." I couldn't argue much with his assessment.

Ridicule of our highest officials, including our president, is standard fare on late night TV comedy shows. Disrespect and irreverence are increasingly characteristics of our society. Nor are they reserved for our highest officials.

In a culture that prizes freedom to the point of fostering disobedience, it is a challenge to remember that the only true freedom is that which Christ gives. And it is even more challenging in such a culture to model the submission that Jesus himself practiced.

Blessed Lord, help me to understand that the greatest self-control is demonstrated in willing submission to You and to others. Through Christ I pray. Amen.

Live by the Spirit

So I say, live by the Spirit, and you will not gratify the desires of the sinful nature (Galatians 5:16).

Scripture: Galatians 5:16-21
Song: "Light the Fire Again"

We began our whitewater rafting trip by paddling up to the very base of Cumberland Falls. The power of pounding water vibrated the boulder-strewn bed of the river. I could feel those vibrations as we worked hard to bring ourselves into the mist of the cascade. As soon as we quit rowing, the boat shot away, caught in the power of the river.

In life, we are always caught by one current or another. The flesh pulls us toward thrills of indulgence. Too late, we see the jagged boulder, feel the surging grip of the hydraulic, and find ourselves caught in a swirling eddy.

When we choose to walk by the Spirit, His leading sweeps us away from the pull of this world. When we are willing to let go of the snares of the flesh, we enter a stream of refreshing.

As long as we dwell in this body of flesh, there will be tension between the two. But in choosing, both deeply and daily, to live by the Spirit, we deaden the draw of a sinful nature.

Yes, we must still row down this river of real life on earth. But the leading of the Spirit is always with the flow of the river of life.

My gracious Father, I renounce the works of the flesh and confess that they are evil and destructive. I choose instead to follow You. Draw me by the power of Your Holy Spirit and lead me by His teaching and wisdom. In the name of my Savior, Jesus Christ, I pray. Amen.

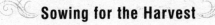

Sowing for the Harvest

Do not be deceived: God cannot be mocked. A man reaps what he sows (Galatians 6:7).

Scripture: Galatians 5:22–6:10
Song: "Bringing in the Sheaves"

I have always been fascinated by the miracle of seeds. As a young kid, I helped plant our garden in southwestern Kentucky. Later, I helped with planting the farm crops. Still later, I planted my own gardens. Always, I waited excitedly for the first showing of the plants.

Even though the first two or four leaves looked nothing like the later leaves, I knew that the beans would soon show their heart-shaped leaves, and the corn would turn tiny first signs into long blades. It seemed impossible that these tiny sprouts could ever turn into anything of note. Eventually, though, the plants would tower over me.

In the blooming, both vine and stalk began to form seeds of the very nature from which they had sprouted. Always we harvested only beans from beans, corn from corn, melon from melon. Never did we plant cockleburs and reap roasting ears. Nor did we ever pull muskmelons off of milkweed.

The refreshing and delicious fruits of the Spirit are harvested when we sow after the Spirit. The seeds of peace and patience, goodness and kindness, will yield the fruits of their kind.

Eventually.

Dear Lord, help me always to stay in step with the Spirit, to plant the seeds of love, joy, peace, patience, kindness, goodness, faithfulness, gentleness and self-control. Help me never give up on doing good for others. Through Christ, amen.

The Infinite Value of Wisdom

Choose my instruction instead of silver, knowledge rather than choice gold (Proverbs 8:10).

Scripture: Proverbs 8:1-11
Song: "Holy Bible, Book Divine"

A college student returned to the family farm for summer break. "Dad, I don't believe in God any longer. I believe a good education will give me all the knowledge and wisdom I need to be successful. How can I believe that an all-knowing God created everything? A wise creator would not have hung tiny acorns on our big oak tree and attached big pumpkins from that scrawny vine over there. If I had created the world, I would have been smart enough to grow acorns on the vine and pumpkins on the oak tree."

As the boy and his father walked under the oak tree, a sudden wind loosened an acorn and it dropped on the young man's head. "Dad," he said, "God must have known what He was doing after all."

The Bible imparts wisdom to all who read it with open hearts and minds. King David had access to the vast wealth of his kingdom, but he wisely valued God's Word more highly than gold and silver. He wrote, "The law from your mouth is more precious to me than thousands of pieces of silver and gold" (Psalm 119:72).

Father, I know money can't buy wisdom. You alone are the source of wisdom. As I meditate on Your Word, grant me wisdom to surmount challenges, make good decisions, and seize opportunities. In Jesus' name, amen.

February 27–29. **Dr. Jim Dyet** is a retired minister and editor. He and his wife, Gloria, have been married 52 years and reside in Colorado Springs. They have three adult children, two granddaughters, and three small dogs. Jim enjoys golf and daily walks with his dogs.

The Richest People on Earth

My fruit is better than fine gold; what I yield surpasses choice silver (Proverbs 8:19).

Scripture: Proverbs 8:12-21
Song: "I'd Rather Have Jesus"

Although the situation was serious, I chuckled. I was boarding a plane at Chicago's O'Hare when a drug enforcement officer pulled me to the side and asked, "Sir, what is your destination?"

"Toronto," I replied.

"Are you a citizen of the United States?" she demanded.

"Yes," I replied.

"I need to see some proof of citizenship."

Thankfully, I had adequate proof of citizenship, but the interrogation continued. "How long will you be out of the country, and what is the nature of your business in Toronto?"

"I will be there for the weekend, and I will be preaching at a church."

"Are you carrying more than $10,000 in cash?"

Unable to suppress a laugh, I assured her I wasn't.

The thought of a preacher carrying $10,000 struck me as funny. I have yet to meet a preacher with that kind of cash.

Nevertheless, all who possess God's Word have a treasure worth far more than $10,000. The Word is able to make others "wise for salvation through faith in Christ Jesus" (2 Timothy 3:15). Let's share the priceless good news liberally.

Father, I am rich because I possess a priceless treasure—Your Word. May I share its message of salvation freely with those who are spiritually bankrupt. In Jesus' name, amen.

Speak a Good Word for God!

Praise be to the God and Father of our Lord Jesus Christ, who has blessed us in the heavenly realms with every spiritual blessing in Christ (Ephesians 1:3).

Scripture: Ephesians 1:3-10
Song: "Praise to the Lord, the Almighty"

A funeral director asked me to conduct a funeral for a man in town who was known to be an apparently "hopeless" alcoholic.

I agreed to conduct the service, but I expected very few mourners to attend. My expectation was almost correct, but I had overestimated the attendance. Not even one mourner attended. When 10 minutes had passed, only the funeral director, a pauper's casket, a dozen empty chairs, and I occupied the little chapel. To his credit, the funeral director said, "I will sit down. Please go ahead and say what you had planned to say."

It was a strange funeral. Zero attendance, except for the funeral director and me. And no eulogy. Apparently, no one had even one good thing to say about the deceased.

The apostle Paul exhorted the Ephesian believers to praise God—literally to speak a good word for God (eulogize Him). Of course, God is eternally alive, but my earthly life will end someday. While I have breath, I ought to speak a good word for Him today and every day. He is good, kind, loving, wise, faithful, truthful, merciful, just, and holy. It will take eternity to praise Him adequately, but we can make today a praise day.

Father, You are perfect and everything You do is perfect. You bless me spiritually and materially every day. I do not deserve the least of Your favors, but Your grace overflows in my life. I will speak a good word for You wherever I go. In Jesus' name, amen.

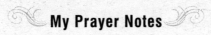

My Prayer Notes

My Prayer Notes

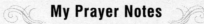